HISTORIC CEMETERIES *of Houston and Galveston*

HISTORIC CEMETERIES *of Houston and Galveston*

TRISTAN SMITH

Published by The History Press
Charleston, SC
www.historypress.com

First published 2023

Manufactured in the United States

ISBN 9781467153966

Library of Congress Control Number: 2023934820

For Sara,
exploring this world with you is simply the absolute best.

For Dad,
thank you for everything. We miss you.

CONTENTS

ACKNOWLEDGEMENTS

One of the first things I manage to do on moving to a new place is find cemeteries. They serve as great landmarks for direction (they rarely, if ever, change, and they don't move about) and as a great way to introduce yourself to local history. When I first moved to Houston in 2011, I grabbed *Historic Photos of Houston* by local historian Betty Trapp Chapman to get a quick lay of the historic land in Houston.

Then I started to explore and hit cemetery after cemetery. My first was the impressive Glenwood. The size and scope of the grounds there is almost overwhelming. Each time I return, I find something I haven't yet seen. Then I found Founders Cemetery, then Olivewood, then tiny little plots and markers I haven't included in this book as they were too far-flung or sparse. Each time, I uncovered something new about the history and culture of Houston. The ever-changing landscape and nature of the surrounding neighborhoods sometimes see the cemeteries change with them or stay stuck in time, a capsule of what Houston once was and where Houston once was.

I would like to thank Ben Gibson, my editor at The History Press, who has provided guidance, assistance and the occasional nudge. Many thanks to Zoe Ames, copyeditor at The History Press, without whom this would be a jumble of words. I'd also like to give a shout-out to Story Sloane, whose photograph collection and knowledge is unmatched outside of museum collections in Houston. I would also be remiss if I did not thank the following people with the following cemeteries for their assistance, information and tips while I explored the history of their landmarks. Marjorie Elhardt, Mike

Cardenas and Kay Tobola with the Glendale Cemetery Association; JoAnn Zuniga with the Archdiocese of Galveston-Houston; and Margott Williams and Jasmine Lee with the Descendants of Olivewood. This book would not have been possible without their influence.

INTRODUCTION

One of the many things I inherited from my parents was a love of exploration. My mother loved to find old, abandoned places, locations that had been forgotten about, places like old cemeteries. This book has a good handful of those but also those cemeteries not forgotten, those still cared for and those still being used. In a city as large as Houston, one cannot go far without stumbling across one. Additionally, one cannot wander into a Houston cemetery and not stumble across a notable figure, such as Howard Hughes or Gene Tierney, or a local celebrity, like Marvin Zindler or Jack Yates.

This book could be so much longer. However, I've left out (most) cemeteries that made it hard to have enough people of notoriety (like Earthman Resthaven Cemetery, where author Donald Barthelme rests) or were too far away, like DJ Screw in Smithville near Bastrop. I'll still get you to stretch your legs a bit. This book covers the entirety of the Greater Houston Area, including out into Fort Bend and down onto Galveston Island. Your trek will cover the resting places of veterans from wars dating as far back as the American Revolution; from periods of national strife, such as the Civil Rights Movement; and from the battle over Texas's Independence and the Civil War. Within each cemetery are heroes, national headliners, forgotten figures and people who made names for themselves under sinister motives and methods, all bringing with them heartwarming and heartbreaking stories.

Right: Multimillionaire Howard Hughes is one of the most notable figures laid to rest in Houston. He earned notoriety as a young man when he inherited his father's company and fortune and then made his own name as a filmmaker, pilot, investor and eccentric. *Courtesy of Library of Congress.*

Below: The Donnellan Crypt is one of Houston's most interesting burial sites. No longer in use, the location still shows evidence of its existence from the mid-nineteenth century. *Author's collection.*

There are some unique locations that deserve longer listings. With this book's limited scope, I couldn't justify keeping some sites—but let's briefly touch on them. Where today's Elder Street Artists' Lofts stand used to be the location of the original city cemetery from 1840. Some graves were moved, ditto the headstones, but during construction projects over the years, burial remains have been uncovered. One surprise was the discovery of bodies wrapped in shrouds, found with dark soil and ceramic shards dating to the seventeenth century. This location is now believed to have been the site of an early settlement, established by King Charles, whose Huguenot inhabitants acted essentially as pirates. Maps of such early settlements have matched up with Buffalo Bayou. The Donnellan Crypt, downtown under the Franklin Street Bridge, once held the remains of Tim Donnellan and his family. Their remains were moved as Houston grew and traffic became a concern; however, the bricked-up crypt remains. Lastly, William Marsh Rice, following his murder by close associates, was cremated and his urn placed inside a monument on the grounds of Rice University, the institution of higher learning that he established.

As you explore, please keep in mind that while some of these cemeteries are historic and only periodically open, they remain cultural and historical keepsakes. Watch where you step and where you sit, and take only pictures. Other cemeteries are perpetual care, meaning that a fund exists to help maintain cemetery grounds, graves, crypts, mausoleums, etc., and the cemetery remains open for many hours nearly every day. These are primarily larger and newer cemeteries. With that comes difficulty in finding the exact locations of some headstones and other landmarks. In these instances, it might be best to stop in at the office or, better yet, to call ahead.

Chapter 1

BETH ISRAEL CEMETERY

1207 West Dallas Street Houston

Located in the Old Fourth Ward of Houston, just west of present-day midtown, Beth Israel Cemetery is in the early stages of a history renaissance. Once a neglected neighborhood, this area is enjoying a new cultural appreciation. Multiple homes are being restored and museums planned on the history and culture of Houston's Fourth Ward and Freedmen's Town. Beth Israel shares its eastern border with Founders Memorial Cemetery, and a branch is located within Woodlawn Cemetery on Antoine Drive, with all records and information located there.

History

Here lie some of Houston's most prominent Jewish residents. Established in 1844 with its first interment, the cemetery predates the founding of the Orthodox Jewish congregation, which is typically the course of action in a new community. Twenty Jewish families came together in the 1840s to dedicate the cemetery, roughly a decade before founding the congregation, as it was one of the foremost obligations in a Jewish community to form a cemetery, because death waits for no one. Beth Israel is not only one of the most historic cemeteries in Houston but also the oldest Jewish institution in the state.

Local Celebrities

Rabbi Hyman Judah Schachtel (1907–1990) famously led Congregation Beth Israel for thirty-two years and served another fifteen years as rabbi emeritus and then as Houston's "rabbi at large" until his death. Rabbi Schachtel arrived in the United States as a child aboard the *Lusitania.* As an adult, he had a pulpit in New York before moving to Houston in 1931 and befriending Lyndon Baines Johnson, for whom he would deliver the inaugural prayer in 1965. He served on multiple boards and organizations but became known to generations of Houstonians through his *Houston Post* columns and a radio show on KODA-FM.

Edna Meyerhoff Levy (1905–2001) moved from Chicago with her family in 1926. Her father, Manuel Meyerhoff, developed Rice Village in the mid-1930s. Here, Edna and her husband, William (1904–1968), started Rice Boulevard Food Market, just west of Rice Institute along an unpaved dirt road. In later years, the store became Rice Epicurean Market, enlarging five times until it could no longer expand. In 1957, the Levys opened a second store in the Tanglewood neighborhood. The business survived William's 1968 death, and Edna continued surging forward, bringing in other members of her family as they grew up. Rice Epicurean Market continues to be wholly owned by the Levy family and has become Houston's oldest family-owned supermarket.

Notable Resident: Ben Taub

Ben Taub (1889–1982) is a familiar name in Houston as both a philanthropist and a medical benefactor. Following service in the First World War, Taub returned to Texas and helped expand the family business, eventually becoming a real estate developer. Additionally, there were few organizations that Taub did not have his hand in, chairing or operating dozens of companies and serving, at one time, on twenty-three boards, including those of numerous medical operations and a predecessor to the United Way. In 1936, Taub donated thirty-five acres of land southeast of downtown to establish a permanent campus for the University of Houston and then helped find more land for the university to fill.

Ben also was instrumental in luring Baylor College of Medicine away from Dallas and into Houston's expanding Texas Medical Center. Never married, Taub spent much of his free time visiting patients in the county hospital. When Houston's new charity hospital opened in 1963, it was named in his honor in recognition of his service. It has since become one of the nation's leading major trauma centers.

Notable Resident: Mitchell Westheimer

If you live in Houston, you recognize this family's name, and if you are visiting, you will likely encounter it at some point in your travels. The Westheimer family plot includes Mitchell "Michael" Louis Westheimer (1831–1905); his wife, Babette "Betty" Hirsch Westheimer (1838–1915); and their eight children. Michael settled in Houston in 1859 and purchased a 640-acre farm just west of the city limits, where both St. John's School and Lamar High School are located today.

Mitchell "Michael" Westheimer was well known in his own time. He started one of the only schools in the area at the time for his own sixteen children, inviting those living nearby to attend also. Today, he is synonymous with traffic in Houston, as the major east–west thoroughfare through town has been bestowed with his last name. *Courtesy of Special Collections, University of Houston Libraries.*

Westheimer married Babette the following year, and together they would raise eight of their own children, three orphans and five children of relatives. With sixteen children under his roof and care, and with no public school system established in the area, Westheimer built a school on his land. He invited those living nearby to join the school. Those attending traveled along the "road to Westheimer's place," passing by the school and the Westheimers' large residence as well as their livery stables and a racetrack. Westheimer was a miller and a hay merchant who built Houston's first streetcars and opened the Houston Livery Stable. In 1895, he allowed the county to build out a right-of-way for a road that stretched away from Houston out to Columbus and Sealy. The "road to Westheimer's place" became Westheimer Road. Today, it is the major east–west thoroughfare in Houston, running west from Bagby Street near downtown Houston for roughly thirty miles.

Notable Resident: Joseph Finger

The Austrian architect Joseph Finger (1887–1953) settled in Houston in 1908, remaining there until his death, and left his mark by bringing modern architecture to Texas. Through a series of early architecture partnerships, Finger designed several hotels throughout the state, including Houston's Ben Milam Hotel and the Texas State Hotel. While his hotels were typically conservative in their designs, many catered to the wealthy and featured uncommon amenities for the time, such as air-conditioning and "running ice water." Finger showed flair in others by employing the Art Deco style, as seen in Temple Beth Israel and over two dozen Weingarten grocery stores.

Additionally, Finger designed several single-family residences. A few homes in the Riverside Terrace neighborhood are marked with his design stylings. Other iconic buildings in Houston of Finger's design are the mixed-use building for the Houston Chamber of Commerce that featured a Levy Brothers Dry Goods storefront, a collaboration with fellow Houston architect Alfred C. Finn; the Jefferson Davis Hospital; the Houston Municipal Airport Terminal (now housing the Houston Air Terminal Museum); the Harris County Courthouse; and the Houston City Hall. He finished out his career in partnership with George Rustay, from 1944 until his death in 1953, after which he was placed in the Beth Israel Mausoleum, a structure of his own design.

Special Features

The Temple of Rest Mausoleum is architect Joseph Finger's iconic Art Deco structure. The intricate design work includes stained-glass windows, bronze ironwork and an elaborate chandelier. Over the years, the chandelier's bulb covers broke off and the bulbs were removed. In order to preserve the original Art Deco design, the search was on to find a glassblower who could replicate the original covers. After some time and many dead ends, the cemetery director tracked down an Austin-area glassblower, Leigh Taylor Wyatt, who said she could have a mold

The Temple of Rest Mausoleum not only holds its creator's remains but also stands as architect Joseph Finger's iconic Art Deco masterpiece. The intricate structure includes this stained-glass window as well as many other features. *Author's collection.*

fabricated and new covers designed. Additional brass work and electrical work was completed, and the 1934 chandelier was lit once again. For this special project, the Congregation Beth Israel was awarded Preservation Houston's Good Brick Award.

Chapter 2

BROOKSIDE MEMORIAL PARK CEMETERY

12747 Eastex Freeway
Houston

Located on the north side of Houston's outer loop, Brookside is almost as far north as Houston Intercontinental Airport. Located in the Aldine area of Houston, the 290-acre Brookside Memorial Park Cemetery heavily resembles a park and is renowned for its majestic oak and pine trees, some of which are over three hundred years old. Except in the oldest section of the cemetery, the old Berry section, where graves date to 1848, you will find no upright markers here.

History

This nondenominational cemetery has served Houston since the 1930s and today features a large and spacious funeral home. It was started by Ira Brooks out of Tulsa, who wanted to get into the cemetery business in Houston. He was bought out by speculator (and non-relative) Pierce Posey Brooks and then eventually by Charles Saunders, a successful salesman and sales manager at Forest Park Lawndale. In 1943, graves from Allen Parkway Village, which was the original Old City Cemetery No. 3, were moved here as were graves from the Episcopal-Masonic Cemetery. The cemetery sections containing walkways are part of the original cemetery grounds, prior to the addition of graves from the other cemeteries.

Located among the majestic oaks and a slew of newer grave sites sits the old Berry section of Brookside Memorial Park Cemetery. This older section, next to the chapel, dates to 1848 and is the oldest section of the cemetery. *Author's collection.*

Local Celebrities

Known as the Wildman from Texas, Therman "Sonny" Fisher (1931–2005) grew up listening to his father sing and play the guitar. After settling in Texas, Sonny formed the Rocking Boys group, influenced by seeing Elvis Presley perform in 1954. His group would appear alongside Elvis as well as George Jones and Tommy Sands in Beaumont and Houston. Combining the blues and country genres, Fisher became a pioneering rockabilly artist in the 1950s. Unable to break past the local circuit, and with an output of only eight songs, he left the music scene in 1965 and dedicated his time and efforts to his floor-laying business. In 1980, a compilation record released in Europe called *Texas Rockabilly* became a hit, leading to a growing interest in the genre and pulling Fisher back into the limelight. He would record an EP of new material and then disappear once again in the 1990s.

Notable Resident: William Daniel "W.D." Jones

William Daniel "W.D." Jones (1916–1974) grew up in the tent city shacks of Great Depression–era West Dallas. While living in the squatter's camp under the Oak Cliff Viaduct, he met Clyde Barrow, six years older than the five-year-old W.D. W.D. lost half of his family to the Spanish flu, and the remaining Joneses would become, and remain, close friends with the Barrows.

W.D. quickly became a fixture at the Barrow service station and with the local police in his mid-teens, collecting license plates for his friend Clyde and brother Marvin "Buck" Barrow for stolen cars. Eventually he would join Bonnie and Clyde on their crime spree, becoming involved during a botched car heist in Temple that resulted in murder. He was wounded during the raid and shootout in Joplin, Missouri, which led him to leave the gang to recover.

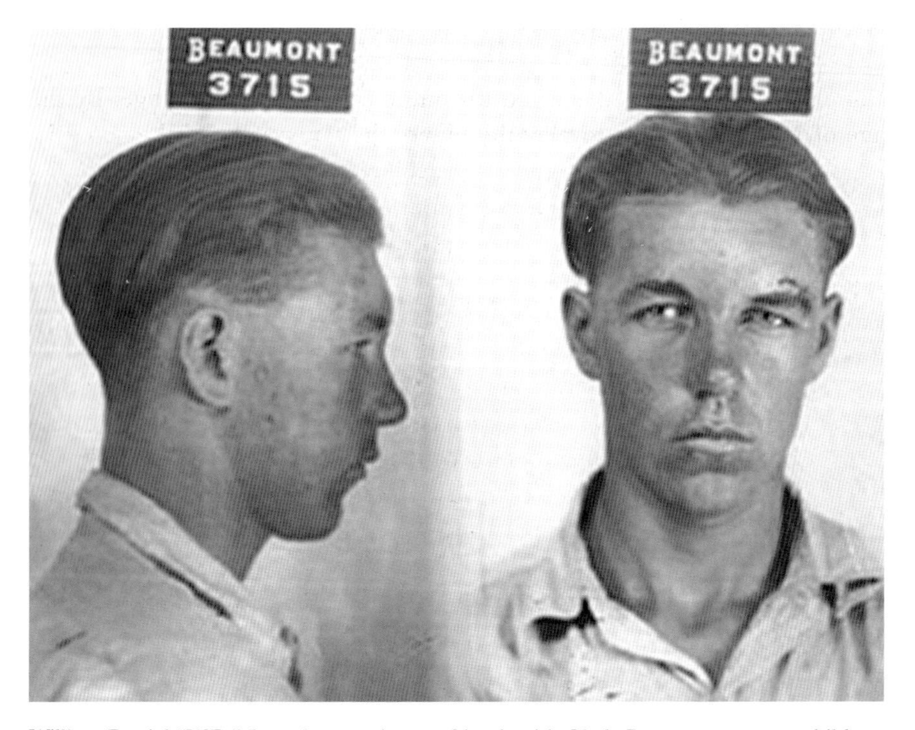

William Daniel "W.D." Jones became instant friends with Clyde Barrow as a young child. Jones would join the rest of the Bonnie and Clyde gang in many of their most notorious outings. He managed to avoid the same fate as his friend and lived the rest of his life in Houston. *Courtesy of Library of Congress.*

He later returned and was present during the wreck that severely injured Bonnie's leg, an injury that plagued her until her death and likely started the downfall of the gang. He managed to escape with Bonnie and Clyde during the Iowa shootout that resulted in Buck's eventual death and Blanche's capture. Once Bonnie and Clyde healed enough from the wounds to travel again, they returned to West Dallas, and W.D. left the gang for good. He tried to keep a low profile but was eventually arrested in 1933 and went up for trial, where he was convicted of murder without malice and of harboring Bonnie and Clyde. He was in jail on the morning of May 23, 1934, when Barrow and Parker were ambushed and killed. Jones spent six years in the Huntsville Penitentiary before being paroled and lived the rest of his life in Houston.

Notable Resident: William "Bill" Wayne Tillman

Bill Tillman (1947–2012) started his music career at a young age. By the age of ten, he was able to play the piano, the tenor sax and the acoustic, electric and electric bass guitars. The following year, he became a paid musician, hitchhiking all over Houston to earn money for his family. During the day, he would attend school. At night, he would join other professional artists to perform.

Over the years, Tillman appeared on CBS's *Salute to Youth*, performed as a featured soloist on recordings by B.J. Thomas and Roy Head and went on a U.S. tour with the Coasters and then Chuck Berry and Bo Diddley, all by the age of twenty-one. He settled in Nashville for a year, performing with Roy Orbison, before returning to Texas and forming Rose Colored Glass in Dallas. They toured with Gladys Knight and the Pips and with Blood Sweat and Tears (for five years) and performed on over fifty live television shows, including *The Merv Griffin Show*, *The Tonight Show with Johnny Carson* and *The Midnight Special with Wolfman Jack*. He played at the 1976 Olympics and multiple national jazz festivals, toured with the Duke Ellington Orchestra and entertained President Bill Clinton, Ross Perot and the United States Navy before his death in 2012.

Chapter 3

COLLEGE PARK CEMETERY

3605 West Dallas Street Houston

Once run down, overgrown, forgotten and intimidating in its appearance, College Park Cemetery has had new life breathed into it—and it shows. College Park once served as the heart of a vibrant, nationally recognized Houston community. Today, it can be found between downtown and the Galleria, just south of Allen Parkway.

HISTORY

If Glenwood Cemetery is the River Oaks of the Dead, then College Park Cemetery would be the Freedmen's Town of the Dead. Founded in 1896, this is one of Houston's three oldest and most historic Black burying grounds, along with Evergreen and Olivewood. Over four thousand people have been laid to rest within College Park. Many of these sites, throughout the 5.2 acres, are now unmarked or unidentifiable.

The cemetery took its name from its neighbor, the Houston Central College for Negroes, which operated across the street from 1894 to 1921. College Park became one of the central burial grounds for African American residents during segregation. In 1998, the Bethel Baptist Church acquired the cemetery, giving the cemetery its first Black owners ever. Since then, sidewalks have been built, markers added and new stones and benches placed on the grounds. In 2012, a new fence, running along Dallas Street, finally enclosed the entire cemetery for the first time.

Local Celebrities

Private Bryant Watson (circa 1882–1917) was killed during the Camp Logan Riot. Private Watson was in Company K, Twenty-Fourth Infantry, and was shot through the right shoulder and once through the back of the neck, the victim of friendly fire. Either shot would have been a fatal one, and his body was found at the intersection of San Felipe and Wilson Streets. Houston police officer Rufus Daniels was killed nearby as well, as were the police horses. A military headstone was added to Private Watson's grave site in 2017.

Following the death of Jack Yates, a prominent minister and the leading African American Houstonian of the late nineteenth century, Ned Pullum (1871–1927) became the pastor of Bethel Baptist Church. The family home he and his wife built, at 1319 Andrews, still stands and is being converted into a museum site. Although laid to rest in a now-unmarked grave, his roots run deep throughout Freedmen's Town: he founded the Carnegie Colored Library, established a brick factory that helped pave the streets of Freedmen's Town and strongly supported Union Hospital, a medical facility for African Americans during segregation.

The Camp Logan Riot of 1917 was a massive uprising of the soldiers in the Twenty-Fourth Infantry. Following poor treatment and then outright violence at the hands of officers in the Houston Police Department, the soldiers decided to strike back. What resulted was the largest military murder trial in history. *Courtesy of National Archives.*

NOTABLE RESIDENT: REVEREND JOHN HENRY "JACK" YATES

John Henry "Jack" Yates (1829–1897) was born into slavery in Virginia. At that time, it was a crime for a slave to learn to read. Despite this, his mother would sneak young Jack into the nearby woods with a Bible and teach him to read. Jack would later marry Harriet Willis; they had eleven children together. When Harriet's master, in 1863, moved her and the children to Texas, Jack stayed behind. It wasn't until after emancipation was announced that Yates finally joined his family.

Jack Yates was born into slavery, learned to read in the woods in secret and married while enslaved. Following emancipation, Yates became one of the most influential figures in Houston's African American community. *Courtesy the African American Library at the Gregory School, Houston Public Library.*

In Houston, Yates served as a drayman by day. By night, and on Sundays, he served as a preacher. In 1866, Antioch Missionary Baptist Church selected Yates to be its first pastor. Under his management, the church functioned as infrastructure for former slaves, teaching them the basics of how to function in the world as free men: how to read, get jobs, understand contracts and more. His influence reached beyond the pulpit, as he was a leader in the creation of both Emancipation Park and Houston Academy.

NOTABLE RESIDENT: RUTHERFORD B.H. YATES

The son of the Reverend Jack Yates, Rutherford attended Bishop College in Marshall, Texas. He earned a degree in printing, returned to Houston to practice his trade and opened Yates Printing and Lithographic Company in 1922 with his younger brother Paul. The two Yates siblings became the first Black entrepreneurs to own and operate a printing company in Houston. Together, they would publish books, bibles, hymnals and newspapers.

Rutherford was also the person responsible for getting the dirt streets of Freedmen's Town, the district where he lived and worked, bricked, and he fought to have a streetcar track laid along what is today West Dallas, the main route into Freedmen's Town. In 1997, the Rutherford B.H. Yates Museum opened to the public. It shares about the story of Yates, the enterprising spirit of those in Freedmen's Town and the history of the famed black neighborhood of Houston.

Notable Resident: First Sergeant Vida Henry

First Sergeant Vida Henry (1875–1917) was a career soldier and the acting First Sergeant of I Company, Third Battalion, Twenty-Fourth Infantry. Henry joined the rest of the Twenty-Fourth on their move from New Mexico to the Jim Crow–heavy city of Houston. Following several encounters and incidents, tensions between the Black soldiers at Camp Logan and the people of Houston, most notably the Houston Police Department, rose to the level of violence. During a series of brutal encounters one day, the

Bryant Watson and Vida Henry were both involved and killed in the Camp Logan Riots. Neither man received a proper headstone until one hundred years following their deaths. Today, both men have been given military headstones denoting their service. *Author's collection.*

soldiers had had enough and began to fight back through an armed uprising, with Sergeant Henry the putative leader. As the "Camp Logan Riot" wound to an end early the next morning, Henry is said to have left the group and committed suicide by his own gun.

However, according to the official records of the coroner and the embalmer, Henry's skull was crushed by a blunt object and he had a stab wound in his chest from either a knife or a bayonet; his official cause of death was listed as "gunshot wound (murder)" due to the riot activities. Some historians question whether Henry was even the leader or if blame was placed on his shoulders merely because he had died and therefore couldn't defend himself or contradict the officially released account.

Notable Resident: John Sessums Jr.

The story of John Sessums Jr. (circa 1848–1928) is a bit of a mystery, especially his early years. The native Texan was likely born into slavery and may be the same Sessums mentioned in newspaper accounts for trying to poison his five children and his wife, accusing her of infidelity. Regardless, Sessums is best known and highly regarded for his drumming prowess. He brought recognition to Houston as a member of several Black militias and as a member of the all-White Houston Light Guard, participating in drill contests across the state. He was a member of the militia for over fifty years, helping it become the best in the country, entering nearly every contest from 1884 to 1888 only to be banned from further competition to give others a chance to win.

John Sessums Jr. was well known for his drumming prowess. Despite the color of his skin, he became a member of not only several Black militias but also the all-White Houston Light Guard. He and the guard were so good that by 1888 they had been banned from further competition to allow others a chance at the title. *Courtesy of Special Collections, University of Houston Libraries.*

Sessums led multiple drill teams before and after the Houston Light Guards, served as a mascot for the Houston Heralds baseball team, organized militia groups for African American youth and remained active in these endeavors for the entirety of his life. In 1910, he was honored with the title of "Perpetual Drummer" by the organization. Nearly two thousand Houstonians, both Black and White, attended Sessum's 1928 funeral, unheard of at the time.

Notable Resident: Isaiah Terrell

Isaiah Milligan "I.M." Terrell (1859–1931) was an early leader for African American education in Texas. Following a stint as a teacher in Anderson, Texas, he was selected to head up the East Ninth Street Colored School in Fort Worth, the first free public school for African Americans. Terrell would go on to help organize the Colored Teachers State Association of Texas, improve teachers' working conditions and advance quality education for African Americans.

In 1915, Terrell became the fifth principal of Prairie View State Normal and Industrial College (now Prairie View A&M University). He oversaw an agricultural extension service and implementation of new studies and vocational education and saw Prairie View become selected as the [a?] teacher training institution. He moved to Houston in 1918 when he was made president of Houston College (a.k.a. Houston Baptist Academy) in the Fourth Ward. In 1923, Terrell became superintendent of the Union Hospital, later securing funding for the new Houston Negro Hospital, where he would become the first superintendent.

Special Features

Following Hurricane Ike's devastation of Galveston, local sculptor Earl Jones descended on many of the trees downed by standing salt water, turning disaster into beauty by wielding his chainsaw like a paintbrush. The over two score of these sculptures that can be found scattered throughout the storm-ravaged East End in addition to works in a variety of media, have brought Earl Jones notoriety. He is also known for his sculpture of Islander boxer Jack Johnson and his works at the College Park Cemetery. One sculpture,

This sculpture was carved from an existing tree by local sculptor Earl Jones. Using a chainsaw as deftly as a painter would a brush, he represented the coming of a new generation with this piece. *Author's collection.*

carved from a tree, uncovered a series of hands reaching out and releasing a bird into the sky above the cemetery grounds, representing the coming of the next generation.

Chapter 4

DE ZAVALA CEMETERY

3523 Independence Parkway
La Porte

Located in the park space directly across the main road leading past the San Jacinto Monument, De Zavala Cemetery covers a scant one acre and contains just over fifty burials. It is located just a half mile north of the monument, across the Houston Ship Channel, next to a parking lot it shares with the spot where Battleship Texas once was docked.

History

Established in 1836, this burial ground was originally located on the De Zavala estate at Zavala Point, home to eventual Republic of Texas vice president Lorenzo de Zavala. The family home was used as a hospital for the wounded following the battle at San Jacinto, which took place just across the bayou. Eventually the cemetery was transported to the state from the estate of Zavala. In the 130-plus years since its founding, a combination of natural forces like tides and erosion, plus man-made disturbances such as the ship traffic on the channel, have wreaked havoc on the property. Eventually the graves became dangerously close to falling into Buffalo Bayou. During the 1960s, an effort to reinter the bodies to their present location was undertaken.

The burial ground of the De Zavala estate sits near Buffalo Bayou along what is now the Houston Ship Channel. Today, it overlooks both the channel and the monument to the Battle of San Jacinto. *Author's collection.*

NOTABLE RESIDENT: MANUEL LORENZO JUSTINIANO DE ZAVALA Y SANCHEZ

Manuel Lorenzo de Zavala served as the Republic of Texas's first vice president. He was born in Mexico, and his political views would cause his exile and eventual relocation to Texas in 1835. He died shortly after resigning his position due to poor health. *Courtesy of Library of Congress.*

Manuel Lorenzo Justiniano de Zavala y Sanchez (1788–1836) served as the first vice president for the Republic of Texas. Born in Mexico, de Zavala was a newspaperman who found his way into politics as a liberal member of the Mexican congress, learned English and became a medical doctor and served as a member of the Cortes in Spain and then as a provincial governor of Mexico. In 1830, his political views would haunt him as he became exiled. After spending time in New York, he immigrated to Texas in 1835, becoming a representative to the 1836 Constitutional Convention. He became a key figure in drafting the Texas Declaration of Independence, signed it and was elected the republic's new vice president. However, having contracted pneumonia shortly after the Battle of San Jacinto, his health was not exemplary. He resigned his position in October 1836 and died at Zavala Point the following month.

NOTABLE RESIDENT: MANUEL FERNÁNDEZ CASTRILLÓN

Manuel Fernández Castrillón (1780s–1836) served under Santa Anna as one of the Mexican dictator's major generals. On March 6, 1836, when nearly all the defenders of the Alamo had been slaughtered, it was Castrillón who implored Santa Anna to spare the lives of a few survivors. Furious that his orders had been disobeyed, Santa Anna instead commanded the survivors be executed immediately. It's possible that this was the group in which David Crockett was killed. Castrillón would continue to serve Santa Anna, leading troops into battle at San Jacinto, near the homestead of an old friend, Lorenzo de Zavala. After Castrillón fell on the battlefield, De Zavala recovered the bullet-riddled body of his friend and honored him with a burial in his own family cemetery across the bayou.

Chapter 5

EVERGREEN CEMETERY

500 Altic Street
Houston

Bordered on three sides by homes and an industrial park on the fourth, Evergreen Cemetery contains some of the most colorful and elaborate grave sites in the city. The main entrance to the cemetery, marked by two large brick towers (which are flanked by two smaller versions of themselves), lies on the cemetery's north side facing North Capitol Street. This entrance was relocated as the Union Pacific rail line interrupted entry to the cemetery any time a train passed by. Peppering the landscape, among its numerous handmade headstones, are some of the finest giant oaks, cedars and hickory trees in the area.

History

While today's Evergreen Cemetery covers fifteen acres, the Evergreen Cemetery Association originally started out with twenty-five acres in 1894 and was touted as "the cemetery of the day." Originally the burials were Anglo-centric; however, that quickly changed, beginning with the Mexican Revolution of 1910. Immigrants and refugees streamed into the barrios east of downtown. As the East End neighborhoods changed demographically, so, too, did Evergreen. Since the 1960s, Evergreen has been almost exclusively used by Houston's Hispanic community, many of whom came to the area seeking jobs at, or around, the Houston Ship Channel.

Evergreen Cemetery boasts some of the most elaborate and colorful grave sites in Houston. This cemetery has a small altar, gifts left behind, mementoes and wind chimes hanging from one of the many trees in the area. *Author's collection.*

Local Celebrity

Ira D. Raney (1878–1917) was a Houston police officer with less than four years under his badge. He was shot and killed during the Camp Logan Riots.

Notable Resident: Maud Griffin

Nicknamed "Tugboat Annie" on the waterways of Houston, Maud Canniff Griffin (1880–1971) was born in Minnesota and lived most of her life in Texas, becoming the first licensed female boat pilot in the state when she was about fifty years old. Maud began her life on boats cooking on her husband's dredge. Then, in 1921, Maud passed her exam to become the only female ship pilot with a license at the time.

Maud gained employment as captain of the *New Brunswick*, operating the ship out of San Jacinto along with her husband, George, and one other man. She became well known and highly respected along the waterways, continuing as a captain following her husband's death in 1924. She hung up her captain's hat and retired in 1932.

Notable Resident: Johnny Kane

Johnny Kane (1904–1936), longshoreman, was killed by scabs during the Gulf Coast maritime workers strike of 1936, an effort to unionize Port of Houston workers. Strikes had become an annual occurrence along the Gulf Coast, and labor conflicts were becoming common. Perceived as corrupt, the leadership of the International Seamen's Union (ISU) brought to maritime workers declining wages and increasingly poor working conditions. All along the Gulf Coast, by March 1935, the seamen and longshoremen had organized, resulting in violent outbreaks, picket lines, arrests and a rising number of killings. In November, the International Longshoremen's Association moved to downtown Houston's Cotton Exchange Building, which quickly became the scene of its own pickets and arrests.

Strikers became particularly interested in one ISU official holed up inside, Wilbur Dickey, who was sharing member information with the police. They attempted to flush him out on December 4, resulting in Dickey firing on them and striking Johnny Kane. Dickey and two companions were beaten by a street mob before being rescued by the police. Kane wasn't so lucky and succumbed to his wounds on December 15. In late January, the violence subsided after the strike ended by union vote in New York City.

Chapter 6

EVERGREEN NEGRO CEMETERY

Lockwood Drive at Calles Street Houston

Being declared a Historic Texas Cemetery by the Texas Historical Commission in 2009 has likely saved this cemetery from being forgotten altogether, much as its neighbor about three blocks south, down Carrol Oliver Way, has been—now a vast empty lot thought to be an abandoned Black cemetery. Only when the grass is cut there can you even see the headstones peeking out of the ground.

HISTORY

The Evergreen Negro Cemetery is located on what was once a cotton plantation. When it was founded, it was the third African American cemetery in Houston, covering just over five and a half acres. Burials date to at least 1887, and among them you'll find former slaves, war veterans and Buffalo Soldiers.

In 1960, the City of Houston expanded Lockwood from Sonora to Liberty, cutting a path right through Evergreen and causing the displacement and reinterment of 490 persons. By the 1970s, both sections of the cemetery grounds were densely overgrown. Since that time, efforts have been made to reclaim and preserve the cemetery. It has received historic status, and the search for Evergreen's disappearing grave sites is ongoing.

Split in half by Lockwood is the Evergreen Negro Cemetery, once the location of a cotton plantation. When it was founded, it served Houston as the city's third African American cemetery. While its upkeep has ebbed and flowed over the years, it has received historic status, and the search for disappearing grave sites continues. *Author's collection.*

Notable Residents: Deputy Arthur Taylor and Detective Isaac "Ike" Parsons

In 1914, two of the few Black officers with the Harris County Sheriff's Office were killed by fellow officers in what was likely a case of mistaken identity.

Deputy Arthur Taylor (circa 1879–1914) was slain in the line of duty on May 24, 1914. He had been appointed as a special deputy under Harris County sheriff Frank Hammon the previous afternoon for the sole purpose of going into the Black community on the near north side of downtown. His goal was to try to apprehend a Black male suspect who was terrorizing the neighborhood with a rifle. Assigned to apprehend the same suspect were officers from the Houston Police Department, including Detective Isaac "Ike" Parsons (1885–1914).

Parsons took it upon himself to go it alone in his attempt to apprehend the suspect. He informed the night police chief that he would not be able to accompany the other assigned officers that night. No one knew that Taylor was heading in for the same purpose. In the darkness, gunshots were heard. Officers approaching the scene at Baron Street near Meadow Street saw a Black man running at them with a gun and fired, killing Deputy Taylor. Detective Parsons rushed to the scene and was struck four times, also dying at the scene. It was later determined that neither Taylor nor Parsons had fired their weapon.

NOTABLE RESIDENT: ALEXANDER K. KELLEY

Former slave Alexander K. Kelley (circa 1846–1928) was a longtime Fifth Ward resident, businessman, railway employee and philanthropist. Despite his lack of formal education, Kelley garnered a reputation through his notable prosperity and civic recognition. Initially working as a porter and later as a coach cleaner on the Houston rail lines, Kelley diligently saved his earnings, buying considerable property in the Fifth Ward. Eventually he gave to and operated dozens of housing projects and rental houses, was a founding member and deacon of the Mount Zion Baptist Church—one of the oldest African American congregations in Houston—and ran a laundry.

Kelley Village, a housing project in Houston, was named for Alexander K. Kelley, a longtime Fifth Ward resident. Throughout his life, he operated dozens of rental houses and housing projects such as this. *Author's collection.*

Kelley's success was reflected in his lifestyle and his legacy. He owned several expensive cars; his family lived in a large, two-story house; he had a chauffeur; and he left a sizable estate for his descendants. Kelley's name has been applied to a street named for him as well as a housing project in Houston. Following his death, the *Houston Informer* stated that he "was connected with almost every movement launched in Houston for the betterment of his group."

Chapter 7

FOREST PARK EAST CEMETERY

21620 Gulf Freeway
Webster

Situated on 143 acres in Webster, Forest Park East Cemetery sits on the west side of the Gulf Freeway, adjacent to the screaming multitudes of vehicles heading toward Galveston and Houston daily. Despite this proximity, the grounds of Forest Park have a serene feel and include several large oak and pecan trees.

HISTORY

Since 1951, the Forest Park East Funeral Home and Cemetery have been a part of the Webster community. Both were founded by James Forbis Eubanks and his family, as were sister sites in other parts of Houston. As the cemetery and community grew, so, too, did the requests for additional services. The plat for the cemetery's columbarium and Chapelview mausoleum is dated June 4, 1962. The on-site funeral home was added a few decades later and conducted its first funeral on October 15, 1989. It now offers a large, cathedral-style chapel, complete with stained-glass windows.

LOCAL CELEBRITIES

Several professional sports figures are buried in Forest Park East. Among the baseball players are TED WILKS (1915–1989), who pitched for a handful of teams, most notably the St. Louis Cardinals and Browns, and PETE RUNNELS (1928–1991), a two-time batting champion who played fourteen seasons for the Senators, Red Sox and Astros. National football running back LOUIS GEORGE "L.G." DUPRE (1932–2001) played for the Baltimore Colts, where he was part of two championship teams, and is neighbors with CHARLIE TOLAR (1937–2003), a short running back for the Houston Oilers known as the "Human Bowling Ball."

NOTABLE RESIDENTS: THE YATES CHILDREN

Buried here are the young children of Andrea Yates: John Samuel (1995–2001), Luke David (1999–2001), Mary Deborah (2000–2001), Noah Jacob (1994–2001) and Paul Abraham (1997–2001). On the morning of June 20, 2001, police responded to an emergency call at the Yates home in Clear Lake. Andrea Yates had made a call to 911 stating she had just killed her children, drowning three of her sons and one daughter. She then picked them up and placed them on her bed, covering them with a sheet. When seven-year-old Noah walked in and saw, he attempted to run but was caught and drowned. Yates had been diagnosed with depression in 1999 following the birth of Noah and was later diagnosed with postpartum depression. She was sentenced to life in prison in 2002. The children were remembered with a candlelight vigil following the tragedy, with a visitation and funeral held in June where their father, Rusty, said his farewell.

NOTABLE RESIDENT: KATIE WEBSTER

Born Kathryn Jewel Thorne (1936–1999), Katie Webster would rise to fame as the Swamp Boogie Queen. Her parents taught her piano but warned her to play only gospel or classical music, not any of that "Devil music." At night, however, Katie would smuggle in an old radio and then craft her own style of music when duly out of earshot of her parents.

When her parents moved to California, a teenaged Katie chose to live with family in southern Louisiana, garnering their permission to play her music at will and earning local notoriety for her music. Eventually she became one of the most requested studio musicians in the area, playing on hundreds of

Katie Webster, known better as the Swamp Boogie Queen, was one of the most requested studio musicians in the Houston area in the 1950s and 1960s, once touring with Otis Redding. She was rediscovered in the 1980s and performed until her death in 1999. *Courtesy of Special Collections, University of Houston Libraries.*

recordings in the 1950s and '60s with people such as Guitar Junior, Lightnin' Slim and Lazy Lester. She toured with Otis Redding as an opening act from 1964 to 1967 but left the tour due to pregnancy. The 1967 plane crash that caused Redding's death caused her to quit the business altogether. Her music saw a resurgence in the early 1980s when blues and rockabilly music were rediscovered in Europe. She toured throughout Europe and America, signed a contract in 1988 with Alligator Records and released her debut album (and two more) with help from Robert Cray and Bonnie Raitt. Katie suffered a stroke while on tour in Greece in 1993. She continued to perform, slowing only slightly until her death in 1999.

Notable Resident: Paul Pritchard Haney

As the voice of the Gemini and Apollo space programs in the 1960s, Paul Haney (1928–2009) was recognizable for people throughout the world. Having previously worked as a journalist, he joined NASA as an information officer shortly before the Soviet Union launched Sputnik. He would serve as the organization's first news director before a transfer to Houston in 1963. There he served as chief of public affairs for the Manned Spacecraft Center (now Johnson Space Center). From 1965 to 1969, he became known to millions of TV viewers as the Voice of Mission Control, providing real-time launch commentary and flight analysis on Gemini and Apollo. Haney retired from the agency on April 25, 1969, over internal disagreements within NASA about information disclosure, three months before *Apollo 11* landed on July 20, 1969—incidentally his birthday. Following NASA, he worked for a variety of news outlets before finally retiring.

If you watched the space race of the 1960s, you would immediately recognize the voice of Paul Haney. He was NASA's chief of public affairs, providing real-time commentary for launches during the Gemini and Apollo programs; however, he retired just prior to *Apollo 11*. *Courtesy of National Archives.*

Chapter 8

FOREST PARK LAWNDALE CEMETERY

6900 Lawndale Street
Houston

Forest Park Lawndale sits near the Idylwood community, in Houston's historic East End. Both the cemetery and the Lawndale Funeral Home are landmarks along Brays Bayou, which empties into Buffalo Bayou at the Houston Ship Channel nearby. Large, native trees pepper the landscape, providing much shade for visitors. This cemetery is listed on Houston's Register of Historic Places.

History

The cemetery was established in 1922. In the past century, Forest Park Lawndale has grown from its initial 49 acres to cover 360 acres, which includes over two hundred thousand burial plots. Not only do grave sites fill the cemetery, but it is also beautifully landscaped and planned. There are three chapels, two conventional mausoleums and two large lakes, plus three lawn crypts.

The Chapel of Angels is notable for its Gothic architecture, the 1922 abbey contains two of Houston's four Tiffany stained-glass windows and Mausoleum Gardens is one of the nation's largest garden-type aboveground mausoleums. Also of note, Forest Park Lawndale participates in the Dignity Memorial Homeless Veterans Burial Program. The program provides for the identification of, and proper military burials for, those homeless and indigent veterans who have no family to claim them.

Local Celebrities

Robert "Bob" Onstead (1931–2004) was the founder and CEO of the Randall's chain of grocery stores around Houston, retiring in 1988. Bob had worked in the grocery industry since he was a child. His son, Randall, took over the top job a year prior to the company selling to Safeway. Bob also served as the chairman of the University Cancer Foundation Board of Visitors (the equivalent of the board of directors at MD Anderson Cancer Center) and started the Houston Economic Council, the precursor to today's Greater Houston Partnership. While he attempted, and failed, to purchase the Astros when they came up for sale, one member of the purchase team, Drayton McLane, would go on to eventually buy the team on his own.

John Henry Kirby (1860–1940) was the largest lumber manufacturer in Texas and the Southern United States throughout much of the late nineteenth and early twentieth centuries. He helped establish the Gulf, Beaumont and Kansas City Railway; the Houston Oil Company of Texas; the Kirby Petroleum Company; and the Kirby Lumber Company. At one time, the latter controlled more than three hundred thousand acres of East Texas pinelands and operated thirteen sawmills. Additionally, Kirby served two terms in the Texas legislature and was a delegate to the 1916 Democratic National Convention.

Thomas Henry Ball (1859–1944) was a Huntsville native, attending Austin College in Sherman and studying law in Virginia. After his admittance to the bar in 1886, he set up practice in Huntsville, where he would serve as mayor from 1887 to 1893. The Texas Democrat would also serve four terms in the U.S. House of Representatives from 1897 to 1905, serve as a delegate to multiple state and national conventions and lose a bid for the Democratic gubernatorial nomination in 1914, becoming instead the general counsel for the State Council of Defense during the First World War. From 1922 until his retirement in 1931, he served as general counsel for the Houston Harbor and Ship Channel. His gubernatorial bid failed after the revelation that he owned a few saloons in the town of Peck, Texas, while running on the prohibitionist ticket. In 1907, the city had changed its name from Peck to Tomball to honor him.

Henry Bizor (1913–1969), blues harpist, is probably best known for backing his cousin, Lightnin' Hopkins, on recordings during the early 1960s. His

Best known as a backup for his cousin Lightnin' Hopkins, Henry Bizor was a talented blues harpist in his own right. He languished in obscurity until a 1960s blues revival uncovered his prowess. *Courtesy of Special Collections, University of Houston Libraries.*

spare, haunting sound has remained timeless, but he dwelled in virtual obscurity until a 1960s blues revival allowed him to be rediscovered. He would go on to have his own solo recording session in Houston between 1968 and 1969. The result, *Blowing My Blues Away*, was shelved until after his April 4, 1969 death.

Joe Henry Eagle (1870–1963), originally from Tennessee, moved to Texas to teach and become a school administrator in Vernon. In 1893, he was admitted to the bar and commenced practice in Wichita Falls, where he served as city attorney until 1895, when he moved his practice to Houston. He was elected as a United State representative in 1913 and served until 1921 and again from 1933 to 1937, starting the latter term by filling a vacancy caused by the death of Daniel Garrett, his neighbor at Forest Lawn. He resumed his practice after a failed bid for a United States Senate seat in 1936.

Bob Horn (1916–1966) was best known for serving as the original host of the television show *Bandstand*, which would go on to greater notoriety as *American Bandstand* under the leadership of Dick Clark. Afterward, Bob became an advertising fixture in Houston until his 1966 death at the age of fifty.

Karla Faye Tucker (1959–1998) was the first woman to be executed in the state of Texas in 135 years. Tucker was sentenced to death for killing two people with a pickax during a Houston burglary. The last woman executed in Texas was Chipita Rodriguez, who was hanged in 1863 during the American Civil War. Tucker was the second woman executed in the United States since 1976, when capital punishment was reinstated, brought to death by lethal injection in Huntsville on February 3, 1998. Her execution and attempts to convert her punishment to life imprisonment have been represented or portrayed by a few musicians, on television and in numerous films.

Karla Faye Tucker, in 1998, became the first woman to be executed in Texas in 135 years. The last, Chipita Rodriguez, was executed during the American Civil War. Additionally, Tucker was only the second woman executed in the United States since 1976. *Courtesy of Library of Congress.*

David Adame (1918–2013) was a civil rights leader who fought for Latin American citizens' rights. The Houston World War II veteran was a member of the League of United Latin American Citizens (LULAC) for more than sixty years. He was influential in launching what would become the Head Start Program and instrumental in inviting President John Kennedy and First Lady Jackie Kennedy to attend a LULAC meeting at the old Rice Hotel on November 21, 1963, the day before JFK's Dallas assassination.

Richard Henry "Dickey" Kerr (1893–1963) was a member of the disgraced 1919 White Sox team that threw the World Series that year. The major league pitcher would later serve as a coach and manager in the minor leagues, having played for the Sox from 1919 to 1921 and avoided implication in the bribery scandal that resulted in permanent bans. He retired after the 1938 season but continued in the sport, including a stint as a pitcher for the Rice Institute Owls and as a manager for the Daytona Beach Islanders, the St. Louis Cardinals class D team. While with the Islanders, he developed a lifelong friendship with a young pitcher named Stan Musial. Kerr recognized Musial's talents as a hitter and convinced him to switch positions, catapulting him to stardom. Kerr would later work for an electric company and, until his death from cancer in 1963, lived in a home purchased for him by Musial.

George Washington Christy (1889–1975) started the Christy Brothers Circus as a young man. Nicknamed "Little Barnum," Christy was very successful, owning several circuses: Lee Brothers, Golden Brothers, Heber Brothers and the Texas Ranch Wild West Show. He claimed to have the largest circus troupe in the world, counting among its ranks 1,250 people, 500 horses, 50 caged animals, 30 lions, 2 railroad cars of camels and elephants, 5 bands, 2 calliopes, 5 mammoth circus rings and a wild beast hippodrome. He was the first to introduce that the circus was coming to town with a long public circus parade. He wintered his operations in South Houston until he sold them in 1930. Afterward he turned to politics and served twice as mayor of South Houston, from 1949 to 1951 and again from 1960 to 1964.

John Saunders Chase Jr. (1925–2012) broke barriers. He was the first licensed African American architect in the state of Texas and the only Black architect licensed in the state for nearly a decade. In 1950, he enrolled at the University of Texas, becoming the first African American to do so at a major university in the south. When no White firm would hire him following graduation, he moved to Houston and started his own. While most of his work is centered in Houston, his buildings can be found throughout the Gulf Coast and in Austin. Among his best works are numerous buildings on the Texas Southern University Campus, including the Martin Luther King Humanities Center, the Ernest S. Sterling Student Center and the Thurgood Marshall School of Law Building.

Alfred Charles Finn (1883–1964) started in the architecture profession with no formal training in 1904 as an apprentice for the esteemed Texas firm

Sanguinet & Staats. Finn worked in the firm's offices in Dallas, Fort Worth and Houston before striking out on his own in 1913. Between 1913 and throughout the 1920s, Finn collaborated on many Houston projects with Jesse Jones, changing the landscape of downtown and starting his career as the project manager for the Rice Hotel project. Finn went on to supervise or design numerous buildings across Texas while continuing work on multiple residential properties throughout Houston. During the 1930s, he and his firm worked for the federal government, and his public buildings included federal buildings, a college administration building, dormitories and the San Jacinto Monument. He became one of the leaders in developing the Art Deco style in Texas and, with Joseph Finger, was one of two leading architects in Houston during this period.

Marcellus Elliott Foster's (1870–1942) family moved from Kentucky to Huntsville, Texas, when "Mefo" (his pen name) was not yet three. Foster graduated from Sam Houston Normal Institute (now Sam Houston State University) in 1890 with another year at the University of Texas in Austin. However, his professional life began before his graduation. He started at the age of fifteen as an apprentice printer at the *Huntsville Item*. In 1895, he joined the *Houston Post*, where, four years later, he became the youngest managing editor of a Texas newspaper. He left the post in October 1901 to start his own publication, the *Houston Chronicle*. For the next quarter century, he would write Our City, his daily column, and achieve acclaim during the 1920s fighting the Ku Klux Klan in the pages of the *Chronicle*. After retiring in 1926, he moved on and became the editor of the *Houston Press*. He continued his fighting status at the *Press* through a new column titled Why, where he covered topics such as prison overcrowding, controversial at the time. Along with his work in the papers, by the time he retired for good in 1941, he had published four books; served on the boards of numerous communities, organizations and companies; and owned the Journal Publishing Company of Beaumont for a year.

Oscar Holcombe (1888–1968) was born in Mobile and raised in San Antonio before moving to Houston at the age of eighteen. At age twenty-six, he started his own construction business, the O.F. Holcombe Company, which thrived, making him a millionaire. Six years later, in 1921, Holcombe won his first term as Houston mayor, serving until 1929. He would serve again from 1933 to 1937, 1939 to 1941, 1947 to 1953 and 1956 to 1958. While he was aggressive about expanding Houston's boundaries and

Left: Albert C. Finn, accomplished Houston architect, struck out on his own in 1913. His designs would change the landscape of Houston's skyline. Along with Joseph Finger, he became one of the Art Deco leaders in the state. The Gulf Building, designed by Finn, is one of his long-standing masterpieces in Houston. *Courtesy of Special Collections, University of Houston Libraries.*

Right: The *Houston Chronicle*, begun in 1901 by Marcellus Foster, has served as Houston's premier outlet for print journalism for over a century. Prior to starting the *Chronicle*, Foster worked for the *Houston Post*, where he became the youngest managing editor of a Texas newspaper at the age of twenty-five. *Courtesy of Special Collections, University of Houston Libraries.*

providing or improving public services ranging from libraries to sewage systems, his administrations were generally considered to be pro-business and conservative.

KENNETH ZIMMERMAN (1913–2008) created architectural designs that are stalwarts of Houston history. Landmarks such as the Astrodome, Rice Stadium and the Jesse H. Jones Hall for the Performing Arts were designed by this career architectural engineer at Walter P. Moore and Associates. Born in west Central Texas, he graduated from Texas A&M University before serving as a second lieutenant in the Army Corps of Engineers. Posted to Oak Ridge, Tennessee, Zimmerman was a property manager

The Eighth Wonder of the World, the Houston Astrodome, was designed by Kenneth Zimmerman. Zimmerman's other designs have become Houston landmarks, if not national ones, and include Rice Stadium and the Jesse H. Jones Hall for the Performing Arts. *Courtesy of Special Collections, University of Houston Libraries.*

aiding the contractors and scientists who were shaping the Manhattan Project and developing the atomic bomb. He would return to his work with Walter Moore following the war. He became the firm's chief engineer and, eventually, its vice chairman of the board before retiring in 1982.

NOTABLE RESIDENT JOHN WILLIAM NEAL

John William Neal (1865–1940) was a lawyer in a grocery firm with Joel Cheek. Along with Neal, Cheek, the originator of a coffee recipe, procured the exclusive rights to serve the new coffee to the guests at Nashville's Maxwell House Hotel, thus giving the brand its name, Maxwell House Coffee. Neal moved to Houston in 1903 and opened a branch of the Cheek-Neal Coffee Company, becoming the distributor of the successful coffee brand to locations throughout the nation. Neal would become not only a coffee magnate but also a successful banker and prominent philanthropist.

NOTABLE RESIDENT: SENATOR LLOYD BENTSEN

Lloyd Bentsen (1921–2006) served his country from the battlefields of World War II to the halls of Congress. Born in Mission, Texas, Bentsen

At one of the most scenic spots in the cemetery, Senator Lloyd Bentsen overlooks Forest Park Lawndale's lake. Following World War II, Bentsen became a long-standing member of Congress, first in the House of Representatives and then the Senate, and eventually ran alongside Michael Dukakis in the 1988 presidential election. *Author's collection.*

graduated from the University of Texas School of Law prior to serving in the United States Army Air Force during the war, where he was awarded the Distinguished Flying Cross for his service in Europe. On returning home to Texas, he won election to the House of Representatives and served from 1948 to 1955.

In the 1970 Democratic senatorial primary, Bentsen defeated incumbent senator Ralph Yarborough before winning against George Herbert Walker Bush in the general election. Bentsen followed up with reelections in 1976, 1982 and 1988. While serving as chairman of the Senate Finance Committee from 1987 to 1993, he was called on by presidential nominee Michael Dukakis to serve as his running mate in the 1988 election versus Bentsen's old Texas foe—and Republican vice president—George Bush and Senator Dan Quayle. Following the failed White House bid, Bentsen would return to the halls of Congress and then serve as secretary of the treasury under President Bill Clinton. In 1999, Bentsen was awarded the Presidential Medal of Freedom and retired to his Houston home, where he passed in 2006.

NOTABLE RESIDENT: RED ADAIR

Paul Neal "Red" Adair (1915–2004), born in Houston, would become an internationally famous American oil well firefighter. His work as an innovator in the highly specialized and hazardous profession of extinguishing and capping oil well blowouts, both land-based and offshore, would bring him world renown. During World War II, Red served in the army's bomb disposal unit, transitioning his expertise and experience to the oil industry following the war's end. In 1959, he founded the Red Adair Co. Inc., battling over two thousand fires.

It was his service fighting the 1962 fire at the Gassi Touil gas field in the Algerian Sahara, nicknamed the Devil's Cigarette Lighter, that shot him to stardom. This 450-foot pillar of fire burned from November 13, 1961, until Adair's team extinguished it on April 28, 1962. He continued to put out high-profile fires throughout the world. At the age of seventy-five, Adair traveled to the Middle East, taking part in extinguishing the oil well fires in Kuwait set by retreating Iraqi troops after the Gulf War in 1991. While he retired in 1993 to his home in Houston, his exploits live on through a portrayal of him by John Wayne in the 1968 movie *Hellfighters*, based loosely on Adair's feats during the 1962 Gassi Touil fire.

Born and bred in Houston, Red Adair would earn international fame as an oil well firefighter. He innovated designs and tools for extinguishing and capping oil well blowouts on land and offshore. He continued as a leader in the field until he was well into his seventies. *Courtesy of National Archives.*

Notable Resident: Hugh Roy Cullen

Hugh Roy Cullen (1881–1957) grew up in poverty in San Antonio with his mother and siblings, abandoned by their father when Roy was four. He worked odd jobs and attempted his hand at various enterprises before losing everything in the Panic of 1907. Things changed in 1915 when he met Jim Cheek, a successful real estate developer who told him about his plan to enter the oil industry, which was booming but still extremely risky. Roy worked for and traveled with Cheek for the next five years.

Things took a downturn when Roy came up dry on three oil rigs, and the constant traveling was ruining his marriage. He decided to stay closer to Houston and search for his own oil. Knowing of a promising salt dome, a sign of oil, Roy followed a hunch on where to drill, gathered up some investments and bought a lease on the land from Gulf Oil. It ended up being a gusher, producing 2,500 barrels of oil a day. While other sites came up dry, investors made 300 percent on return. Roy's success would find its way into the Houston coffers. He and his wife, Lillie, made numerous contributions to the new campus of the University of Houston; established the Cullen Foundation, one of Houston's largest philanthropic organizations; donated land that would become Texas Southern University; and helped fund an expansion and renovation of part of Southwestern University in Georgetown, Texas.

Notable Resident: Mellie Keenan Esperson

Mellie Keenan Esperson (circa 1870–1945) was born in Kansas and moved to Oklahoma as a young woman. There she met Denmark native Niels Esperson (1857–1922), who was involved in Oklahoma real estate and business. After they married, Niels found little success in Oklahoma, Kansas and Colorado, so the couple moved to Houston in 1902. Niels would become a developer of the Humble oil field, and Mellie learned the oil business along with his trajectory. They would diversify their money in Houston into real estate and a multitude of business efforts. Sadly, Niels Esperson died in 1922, but he left his wife with quite an inheritance. She wasted little time.

Mellie's first project was the construction of the John Eberson–designed Majestic Theater, which opened in 1923. The following year, Mellie initiated plans for an office building that Niels had envisioned for property downtown, turning the idea into a memorial to her husband, the thirty-two-story Niels Esperson Building at Travis and Rusk. She called on Eberson again, and his brother Drew, to design an adjoining complementary structure. Completed in 1941, the nineteen-story Mellie Esperson Building is similar in style and, while separate from the Niels, adjoins it on most floors. Esperson had a hand in many locations throughout Houston past these two landmarks, lending support to the development of the Houston Ship Channel, the Museum of Fine Arts, the Houston Symphony and more.

NOTABLE RESIDENT: SAMUEL JOHN "LIGHTNIN'" HOPKINS

Samuel John "Lightnin'" Hopkins (1912–1982) has been ranked as one of the hundred greatest guitarists of all time (*Rolling Stone* listed him as no. 71 in 2010). From the time he was a child, he was immersed in the blues. His mentors included Blind Lemon Jefferson, his older cousin Alger "Texas" Alexander and another cousin, blues guitarist Frankie Lee Sims.

During the mid-1930s, Hopkins found himself incarcerated in Sugar Land, at the Houston County Prison Farm. Following his release, he moved to Houston in an unsuccessful attempt to break into the music business. By the early 1940s, Hopkins was back in Centerville working as a farmhand. In 1946, Sam took another shot at Houston and was discovered by Los Angeles's Aladdin Records. Accompanied by pianist Wilson Smith, the duo traveled to Los Angeles and recorded a dozen tracks in their first session, dubbed by an executive "Lightnin'" and "Thunder." Hopkins would record again for Aladdin, then later Gold Star Records and SugarHill Recording Studios in Houston, rarely performing outside the state during the late 1940s and '50s.

When lists are issued about the greatest this and that, Lightin' Hopkins consistently lands as one of the greatest guitar players of all time. He wouldn't reach the height of his fame until the 1960s, after years of playing consistently. *Courtesy of Library of Congress.*

Then, in the late 1950s and early 1960s, Lightnin' Hopkins leapt to the national stage. On October 14, 1960, Hopkins made his debut at New York's iconic Carnegie Hall alongside folk icons Joan Baez and Pete Seeger, thrusting him into national view. Following this, he recorded *Mojo Hand* and continued releasing albums and touring internationally well into the 1970s. In 1982, Lightnin' Hopkins died of esophageal cancer in Houston, at the age of sixty-nine. The *New York Times* declared him "one of the great country blues singers and perhaps the greatest single influence on rock guitar players." He was inducted into the Blues Foundation Hall of Fame in 1980.

Notable Resident: Jesse Jones

Jesse Jones (1874–1956) was born in Tennessee but became one of Houston's most influential figures in the mid-twentieth century. Jones managed his father's factories starting at a young age and by nineteen had moved to manage his uncle's lumberyards. Shortly thereafter, he opened his own lumberyard and moved to Houston, where he garnered a foothold in industry and real estate.

Jones helped push forward Houston's commercial enlargement through his own involvement in real estate, commercial building and banking, overseeing the start-up of numerous mid-rise and skyscraper office buildings, hotels, apartment buildings and movie theaters and eventually wielding majority control over the *Houston Chronicle*. His power helped expand the influence of the Port of Houston and the Houston Ship Channel. He was tapped by President Woodrow Wilson to head a division of the American Red Cross, and he helped bring the Democratic National Convention to the city in 1928.

Jones's appointment to the finance commission was a central catalyst of the Democratic Party's New Deal of the 1930s, showing the country that, behind President Franklin Roosevelt (and possibly not even him), no one held more power in the country than Jesse Jones. During Roosevelt's presidency, Jones would turn the commission into the biggest bank in the United States, becoming responsible for numerous reforms to the landscape of American finance and politics, eventually culminating in his appointment as the secretary of commerce.

With his wife, Mary Gibbs, Jones established the Houston Endowment Institution, a highly influential funding organization to this day. In addition to this legacy, he lives on in the numerous buildings named for him, multiple buildings still standing that saw his direct and indirect influence, a new plant for the *Chronicle*, the relocated ten-story HQ building for Texaco, a reconstructed seventeen-story Rice Hotel and the Gulf Building, along with investments in Dallas, Fort Worth and beyond.

NOTABLE RESIDENTS: DOMINIQUE AND JOHN DE MENIL

Dominique Isaline Schlumberger de Menil (1908–1997), a prominent Houston philanthropist and patron of the arts, along with her husband, John de Menil (1904–1973), provided a legacy to Houston's art landscape. Born in Paris, France, Dominique's father was a physicist whose technology became essential for oil drilling. His company, Schlumberger, continues operating to this day in Houston and around the world.

Dominique studied at the University of Paris (Sorbonne) and, in 1930, met Jean (anglicized later to John) de Menil at a party. They married the following year. John, a Franco-American businessman, philanthropist and art patron, was the founding president of the International Foundation for Art Research in New York, studying political science in college and graduating with a degree in law. The couple had five children between 1933 and 1947. Due to the escalation of World War II, the anti-fascist Menils left France for the United States in January 1941, permanently settling in Houston, which had long housed some of Schlumberger's company operations.

The Menils' serious interest in art and collecting began in the mid-1940s. Their River Oaks home, commissioned in 1948 by architect and Museum of Modern Art architecture curator Philip Johnson, is considered the first building in Texas in the International Style. Their influence over and infusion of money into Houston's art scene is unrivaled. Due to their impact, primarily through Dominique, Houston saw the creation of a master plan for the University of St. Thomas; the establishment of the Menil Foundation; the commissioning of many Mark Rothko paintings and their later inclusion in the Rothko Chapel; and the creation of the Menil Collection, the Cy Twombly Gallery and the Byzantine Fresco chapel (until 2012, when the frescos were returned to Cyprus).

Chapter 9

FOUNDERS CEMETERY

1217 West Dallas Street
Houston

Located in Houston's historic Fourth Ward, this property was near the edge of Houston when it was founded in 1836. A designated Historic Texas Cemetery by the Texas Historic Commission, the cemetery is easy to find with its large, gated entry and the brick wall and wrought iron fence surrounding it. It also lies adjacent to the Beth Israel Cemetery at the southwest corner of West Dallas and Valentin.

History

Founders Cemetery—also known as Founders Memorial Park, originally City Cemetery—was established in 1836 and opened in conjunction with the establishment of the city of Houston. Located on land settled by the Allen Brothers, a conservative estimate of the number of burials runs well over 850 graves under the two-acre site. Many early influential Houstonians, along with several Republic of Texas veterans, are buried here. Numerous mass burials and, along with them, unmarked graves, are also located here due to recurring yellow fever, cholera and smallpox epidemics. Deaths were occurring in Houston so quickly and in such great numbers that funeral establishments couldn't keep up. Bodies were dumped unceremoniously into long trenches and covered.

Located a short distance from, and in the shadows of, downtown Houston, Founders Cemetery is the final resting place for countless city founders as well as numerous Republic of Texas figures. It's a veritable who's who of early Houston and Texas individuals. *Author's collection.*

Founder's Cemetery received renewed attention in 1936, the centennial of Texas's Republic. It was restored by the San Jacinto Centennial Association, which placed twenty-eight Texas Centennial monuments throughout the cemetery. *Author's collection.*

In April 1936, the cemetery received renewed attention. With its centennial, it was officially renamed Founders Memorial Park and was restored by the San Jacinto Centennial Association. The association placed twenty-eight Texas Centennial monuments, summarizing the biographies of veterans of the Battle of San Jacinto. Restoration and upkeep have ebbed and flowed over the years. In recent years, as the neighborhood surrounding the cemetery has received renewed attention and efforts, so, too, has the cemetery. So far, 130 individual graves have been identified in Founders Memorial Cemetery.

Local Celebrities

John W. Moore (circa 1797–1846), Texas Declaration of Independence signatory, arrived in Texas in 1830, settling in the Harrisburg municipality. The following December, he was elected as the *comisario* of the precinct of San Jacinto. Moore was a friend of William B. Travis and was present when Travis's forces forced Antonio Tenorio's capitulation at the fort at

Anahuac in 1835. Later that year, he served as a delegate from Harrisburg to the Consultation and was one of three representatives from there at the Convention of 1836. He also was elected captain of the Second Militia District, sheriff of Harrisburg Company, founding trustee of the Harrisburg Town Company and alderman of the city of Houston.

REBECCA LAMAR (UNKNOWN–1839) was the mother of the Republic of Texas's president Mirabeau B. Lamar. She died at Oak Grove, their estate in Houston. In addition to Mirabeau, she and her husband, John Lamar Jr. (incidentally her first cousin), had eight other children. Prior to their move to Texas, they raised their family at Fairfield, their family plantation near Louisville, Georgia.

NOTABLE RESIDENT: JOHN KIRBY ALLEN

Houston cofounder John Kirby Allen (1810–1838) was an influential figure in the formation of not only Houston but also the Republic of Texas. He and his brother Augustus moved to New York City in 1827 and then moved together in 1832 to Texas, arriving first in Galveston and then Saint Augustine before falling in with a group of Nacogdoches entrepreneurs. The Allen brothers started operating as land speculators and, instead of joining the army when the revolution reared its head, engaged in the private business of keeping supply channels open and attempting to protect the coast.

Despite rumors of privateering, John was elected to represent Nacogdoches County to the first congress of the Republic of Texas. During his term, the Allen brothers founded the city of Houston, continuing to operate a shipping business. While in congress, John successfully lobbied for the newly founded city to be named the capital of the republic, which would give Houston the boost it needed to survive the first few years throughout development, allowing it to take hold. His influence and expertise with founding Houston led to his election to the board of directors of the Galveston City Company, chartered by the republic to establish the new island city. Never married, John Kirby Allen died of congestive fever in August 1838 in Houston and is buried in Founders Cemetery along with his siblings and parents.

Notable Resident: Henry Livingston Thompson

During his brief tenure as the second commander of the Texas navy, Henry Livingston Thompson (unknown–1837), led the Yucatán Expedition. Held during the summer of 1837, it was one of the navy's most spectacular and controversial campaigns. The navy, a very small fleet, inflicted heavy damage on the Mexican navy as well as the shipping and coastal towns they held. South of the Rio Grande, this navy became known as *los diablos Tejanos*: the Texas Devils. President Sam Houston opted for the navy to have a purely defensive posture in Texas waters, but Secretary of the Navy Samuel Rhodes Fisher and Thompson instead opted to be more aggressive. They decided to break the blockade Mexico held in Texas. In doing so, they battled with Mexican brigades and raided and claimed possession of several Mexican islands before Thompson's own ship, the *Invincible*, was destroyed beyond salvage by storms. Eventually, due to their actions, both Fisher and Thompson were forced to resign. Thompson was threatened with court-martial but died prior to any court proceedings.

Henry Livingston Thompson's grave is marked by one of the twenty-eight Texas Centennial monuments erected throughout the cemetery. Thompson served the republic as the second commander of the Texas navy. *Author's collection.*

Notable Resident: James Collinsworth

A lawyer and jurist who signed the Texas Declaration of Independence, James Collinsworth (1802–1838) held the favor of, and brought with him to Texas, numerous leading Tennessee politicians such as Andrew Jackson and Sam Houston. From 1829 to 1834, Collinsworth served as the United States district attorney for the Western District of Tennessee but moved to Matagorda, Texas, in the Brazos Municipality to begin a law practice the following year. There he served as a representative to the Convention of 1836, where he signed the declaration and introduced and guided to adoption a resolution making Sam Houston the commander in chief of the Texas army.

Collinsworth helped draft the constitution for the new republic at the convention and was appointed by Sam Houston as his aide-de-camp. His actions were commended by General Thomas Rusk for bravery and chivalry following the Battle of San Jacinto. He stayed in politics following the war, briefly serving as acting secretary of state before being commissioned to the United States to seek assistance for possible annexation due to his previous relations with President Andrew Jackson. Collinsworth failed in his efforts. He served in the Republic of Texas's senate and as its first chief justice; helped organize the Texas Railroad, Navigation and Banking Company; and helped found the city of Richmond in Fort Bend County. In 1838, Collinsworth became a candidate, along with Mirabeau Lamar and Peter Grayson, for the presidency of the republic. However, following a full week of drunkenness, he either fell or jumped off a boat in Galveston Bay and drowned. When his body was finally recovered, it lay in state in the republic's capital, his being the first Masonic funeral ever held in Texas.

Notable Resident: Isaac N. Moreland

Republic soldier and jurist Isaac N. Moreland (unknown–1842) moved to Texas in the fall of 1834 from Georgia, establishing himself in Anahuac before moving on to Liberty, where he served as the secretary of the ayuntamiento (essentially the town council or municipality). Moreland was an early leader of breaking away from Mexico, first becoming one of the four signatories of the Liberty Resolutions in 1835 and then authoring the Anahuac Resolutions less than a month later. As tensions escalated, he served as the Texans' vocal opponent to Mexican officials. That October, he joined the Texas army, finding himself appointed as captain of the First Regiment of Infantry in the regular army by Sam Houston. At the Battle of San Jacinto, he helped man the "Twin Sisters" cannons under Lieutenant Colonel George Washington Hockley.

Following the war, Moreland was assigned to command Fort Travis at Galveston, with a promotion to major and then commandant of the garrison. He served there until his discharge in 1837. On moving to

Houston after his service, he went into partnership with David Burnet in a law practice. Eventually, he earned an appointment as chief justice first of the Second Judicial District and then of Harrisburg, a post he held until his death in 1842. While his burial site is now marked, he was initially buried in an unmarked grave.

Chapter 10

GALVESTON BROADWAY CEMETERY HISTORIC DISTRICT

Broadway Avenue
Galveston

On entering the island from Houston, whether you are headed to the Strand or down to the Seawall and beaches, you will find yourself traveling along Broadway, Galveston's primary thoroughfare, lined with business and, eventually, stately Victorian homes, gardens and lush landscaping. One of the major features along this route is the Broadway Cemetery District, located along this pathway.

History

Covering an area just over fifteen acres, this six-block collection of seven cemeteries stretches between Broadway and Avenue L and Forty-Third to Fortieth Streets. Here you will find an estimated twelve thousand grave markers. However, urban burial grounds like this tend to bury deep; the graves are three layers deep here. There are likely more than three times more bodies than there are markers to be found.

The first Anglo settlers on Galveston sought to bury their dead in a proper place. Originally, as people died, the bodies were buried in the dunes. However, time and erosion proved to make this method unsustainable. During an 1839 yellow fever epidemic, nearly 250 lives were lost, making it clear that a more permanent burial ground was needed. The Old City Cemetery was opened as part of the original town charter in 1839 and was joined by an adjacent potter's field. Additional yellow fever epidemics struck the island from 1839

Visitors to Galveston's Broadway Cemetery District are visiting seven different cemeteries. Each of these is located adjacent to the next, separated by a low brick wall. Each is denoted by its own signage or entry gate, such as the gate for the Hebrew Benevolent Society Cemetery, founded in 1868. *Author's collection.*

to 1867, resulting in five additional cemeteries throughout the nineteenth and twentieth centuries. Today, visitors to the district see seven cemeteries: the original Old City Cemetery (1839) was joined with the potter's field (1839), also known as the Oleander Cemetery, and Evergreen (1839), which became the Old Cahill Cemetery in 1867, and then, later, the Old Catholic Cemetery (1844) and the Episcopal Cemetery (1844), the Hebrew Benevolent Society Cemetery (1868) and, finally, the New City Cemetery (1900).

Local Celebrities

Dr. Thomas Joseph (1823–1905) came to Houston from Hartford, Connecticut, in 1841 with his mother, Annis, and the family of his uncle Alexander Edgar. During his time in Galveston, Joseph was admitted to the bar, became a Democratic Party leader on the island and served as chief justice (the then-equivalent of county judge), mayor, state legislator and senator. It's possible that Joseph is buried over the top of his mother's site in Trinity Episcopal Cemetery, which, like others, was lost following several storms.

Wilbur Cherry (1820–1873) left Oswego, New York, at the age of fifteen to join the Texas Revolution. On November 21, 1835, Cherry joined Captain Andrew Briscoe's company of Liberty volunteers and participated in the siege at Bexar. He would stay in the military after the revolution, joining and remaining in the Army of the Republic of Texas until the early 1840s. Later he worked as a printer in Austin and Liberty before moving to Galveston in 1843. There he became a publisher of the *Galveston Weekly News* and, later, the *Galveston Democratic Journal*. At the time of his 1873 death, he was working as a printer at the *Galveston Weekly News*.

Major John Melville Allen (circa 1798–1847) enlisted in the United States Navy as a young man. Not much is known about his life at that point, but it is said he left the service to fight in the Greek War of Independence against the Ottoman Empire and was with the famed British poet Lord Byron when he died in 1824 at Missalonghi. Allen had returned to the States by 1835 and met exiled Mexican general José Antonio Mexía in New Orleans, eventually assisting him in his scheme to reestablish the Mexican Constitution of 1824, known as the disastrous Tampico Expedition, with Mexía, Allen and some of their coconspirators narrowly escaping capture. Allen would participate in the revolution as a cavalryman, joining the army as it retreated to Gonzalez and fought at San Jacinto, distinguishing himself through his fighting skills and for stopping the massacre of defeated Mexican soldiers. After his service, he settled in Galveston, where he was elected in 1839, again in 1841 and then from 1843 to 1845 for three consecutive terms as the city's first mayor. He would serve as justice of the peace for Galveston. Allen led efforts to ease residents' suffering during yellow fever epidemics; advocated for the creation of a hospital, fire services and a jail; and sought reforms for the city's cemeteries. When Texas was annexed in 1846, President James K. Polk appointed Allen as the U.S. marshal for the Eastern District of Texas, a post he held until he died in 1847. On his passing, Galveston held one of the biggest funerals in its history before laying him to rest in the Episcopal cemetery.

Noah Noble John (1817–1892) survived three shipboard disasters before perishing at the age of seventy-five and being laid to rest in Galveston's Old City Cemetery. He managed to escape death during the sinking of the *Brownsville*, emerged from the burning of the *Stare State* and walked away from the explosion of the *Farmer*.

Newton Taylor may have been one of the most beloved characters in Galveston. The island's gravedigger, Taylor was known for attending funeral services, pumping the organ bellows and performing magic tricks for children. *Courtesy of Special Collections, University of Houston Libraries.*

NEWTON TAYLOR (1831–1905), the gravedigger, was a beloved Galveston figure, digging hundreds of graves and attending the funeral services. He was known for pumping the organ bellows at Trinity Episcopal Church as well and was called Uncle Newton' by the children of Galveston, for whom he performed magic tricks. One of his signature stylings was a silk top hat, worn every day to work.

Lawyer and politician GEORGE CAMPBELL CHILDRESS (1804–1841) was the principal author of the Texas Declaration of Independence. He had been elected as the Milam representative to the convention, along with his uncle Sterling C. Robertson, to whose colony he moved in January 1836. While he tended to his duties in Texas, he remained separated from his family, who lived elsewhere. Childress's debts mounted, he failed three times to establish a law practice and as his loneliness for his wife, Rebecca, and their three children increased, his outlook and hopes for the future faded. On October 6, 1841, Childress slashed his abdomen with his Bowie knife, resulting in his death. He was buried in an unmarked grave in the city cemetery. Childress was one of three Texas founding fathers to die by suicide, the others being Anson Jones, by a self-inflicted gunshot wound, and Thomas Rusk, who committed suicide in Nacogdoches. A headstone monument was erected in Trinity Episcopal Cemetery by the State of Texas in his memory.

DR. GREENVILLE DOWELL (1822–1881) moved to Texas in 1853, setting up his medical practice and then serving as a surgeon in the Confederate army in Galveston. Dowell was instrumental in the founding of the Texas Medical

College and Hospital and the *Galveston Medical Journal*, the first of its kind in the state. A noted surgeon, he designed several surgical instruments and became a leading authority on the treatment of yellow fever.

A sea captain's son who became a sailor, fourteen-year-old LENT MUNSON HITCHCOCK (1816–1869) left Connecticut and joined the Texas navy around 1836. His duties would bring him to Galveston, where he later settled and served as the city's harbormaster, treasurer and alderman and as a Confederate army volunteer. Hitchcock played a prominent role in Galveston's early development and was honored with the naming of a nearby town for him in 1891.

NOTABLE RESIDENT: JOHN BANKHEAD MAGRUDER

John Bankhead Magruder (1807–1871) served as a soldier in three armies: those of the United States, the Confederate states and Emperor Maximilian of Mexico. Magruder was appointed to the United States Military Academy at West Point in 1826, graduating in the class of 1830, and rose through the ranks over the next few decades, serving during the Second Seminole War and then with Winfield Scott's army in Mexico and recognized for his service at the Battle of Cerro Gordo and the storming of Chapultepec.

John Magruder was a lifelong soldier. He served in three armies during his career, those of the United States, the Confederate states and Emperor Maximillian of Mexico. In 1863, he recaptured Galveston and dispersed the Union blockading fleet, an act that caused him to be buried in Galveston, the site of his biggest success on the field of battle. *Courtesy of Library of Congress.*

On April 20, 1861, Magruder resigned from the United States Army, opting to support his home state of Virginia in its efforts to establish the Confederate States of America. As a result, he was commissioned a brigadier general and was quickly promoted to major general. His service in the Confederate army started out with mixed reviews. Reassigned to the command of the District of Texas, New Mexico and Arizona following the Seven Days Battles, he arrived in October 1862 and assumed command in late November with headquarters in Houston. His later service was noted through the recapture of Galveston on January 1, 1863, and the dispersal of the Union blockading fleet. Despite his success and popularity, on August 7, 1864, Magruder was transferred to command the Department of Arkansas before returning the following March with just enough time to witness General Edmund Kirby Smith surrender the Trans-Mississippi Department at Galveston on June 2, 1865.

Following the war, Magruder offered his service to Emperor Maximilian in Mexico. Following the collapse of the imperial forces and the subsequent execution of the emperor, he returned to Texas. Magruder made his home at his former headquarters of Houston in 1867. He spent the rest of his days there. Instead of near his home in Houston, it was decided to bury him at the Trinity Episcopal Cemetery, near the scene of his greatest military achievement.

Notable Resident: Lieutenant Commander Edward Lea

Edward Lea (1837–1863), native of Baltimore, entered the United States Naval Academy at Annapolis in October 1851, graduating as a midshipman in June 1855. When the Civil War broke out, Lea was aboard the *Hartford*

Seen here is the Confederate ship *Bayou City* capturing the *Harriet Lane* during the Battle of Galveston. During the capture, Union lieutenant commander Edward Lea was fatally injured. His father, a Confederate major of artillery, saw the capture and raced to the ship, only to find his son dying. *Courtesy of Library of Congress.*

and then reassigned to the *Harriet Lane* before finding his service in the Gulf Blockading Squadron and as a part of the 1862 capture of New Orleans.

That fall of 1862, Lea, now a lieutenant commander, and the *Harriet Lane* were sent to blockade Galveston, helping to secure its capture that October during the Battle of Galveston. The occupation didn't last long. Confederate forces retook Galveston on New Year's Day 1863. Lea, serving as the first officer of the *Harriet Lane*, was wounded in both the abdomen and side. His father, Albert Miller Lea, was serving as a major of artillery in the Confederate army and witnessed the capture of the *Harriet Lane* by the Confederate gunboat CS *Bayou City* from shore. He rushed to the ship only to find his son dying. Lea was buried at the Trinity Episcopal Cemetery in Galveston. When a relative suggested that Lea's remains be reburied at the Green Mount Cemetery in Baltimore, next to his mother, his father, Albert, refused. He stated his son would have preferred to remain where he had fallen in battle.

Notable Resident: Major Leon Dyer

Leon Dyer, born Feist Emanuel Heim (1807–1883), immigrated to Baltimore in 1812 from Germany and opened a meatpacking business. Before moving to New Orleans to open a branch of the family packinghouse, Dyer had been elected a trustee of the Baltimore Hebrew Congregation and was involved in the 1835 Baltimore Bank Riots.

Dyer joined the military while in Louisiana, participating in the Second Seminole War in Florida and then being appointed the regional quartermaster of the Louisiana volunteer militia. In April 1836, he met General Thomas Jefferson Green and joined the Texas War of Independence, arriving in Galveston later that month to restock General Houston with supplies. The following month, he was appointed a major and saw active service helping to clear western Texas of Mexican troops. In January 1837, Dyer was assigned the task of escorting General Santa Anna to Washington, D.C.

Following the revolution, Dyer returned to Baltimore from 1840 to 1845 and received a Hays County land grant for his service to the republic. Afterward, he lived throughout the States, in London and in Germany, marrying and having children along the way. He died in Louisville and was returned to Galveston to be buried at the Hebrew Benevolent Society Cemetery.

Eerie Tales

The Haunting of Thomas "Nicaragua" Smith

While his early life is uncertain, it is believed that Thomas Smith was born in New York. The ex-Confederates who served in Galveston with him knew him only as Nicaragua. He had traveled south during the mid-1850s, a bit of a fortune fighter, joining William Walker's Filibusters in 1856 bound for Nicaragua, which earned him his sobriquet. At some point in 1860, he arrived on Galveston Island. Following the start of the Civil War, in April 1861, there was a series of burglaries along the waterfront. Smith and a few other drifters were arrested, marched to the Central Wharf and loaded aboard a steamer set for Houston with orders never to return. Instead, Smith joined a Confederate artillery battery, was stationed in Galveston on Pelican Island and found himself unsuited for military life. He stole a boat, rowed out to the Union blockade "Santee" and surrendered, whereupon he became a prisoner of war and was sent to New Orleans.

While there, Smith convinced his "captors" that he was born in the north and was loyal to the Union and was allowed to enlist in Colonel E.J. Davis's First Texas Regiment of Union volunteers. Davis's federal transport *Cambria* then found itself off Galveston. The crew looked to bring ashore a new pilot, and when one did not arrive, the captain sent six seamen, including Smith, to bring one back. Smith was immediately recognized as a deserter and arrested. On January 6, 1863, Nicaragua Smith was tried for desertion before a drumhead court martial.

Smith swore he had never been in Galveston but was well recognized and soon sentenced to death before a firing squad. Two days later, he was loaded in a wagon beside his coffin and carried out to the cemetery to a pre-dug grave. Six Confederate soldiers aimed; Smith cursed them, requested to be buried face down and was shot. Reports say his body was riddled with bullets before he fell and again while in the coffin, dead, buried where he fell into an unmarked grave. Rumor has it that if you hear a voice screaming loudly in the cemetery, especially in January, it's probably Nicaragua Smith.

The Murders of Elize Alberti

The Alberti family is buried in one of the oldest cemeteries on the island, the Episcopal. Among the headstones is that of Elize "Lizzie" Roemer Alberti,

Lizzie Alberti, the "demented mother," murdered four of her children in 1894. In what was likely a horrible case of postpartum depression, Alberti suffered increasingly following the birth of her first child in 1884 and after subsequent births. The deaths of other children likely just compounded her state of mind. *Author's collection.*

"the demented mother," according to newspapers in the late 1890s. In 1894, Lizzie murdered four of her children. In 1884, the firstborn child of Louis and Lizzie, also named Louis, died of lockjaw at the age of seven. That same year, Caroline was born. Less than a year later, Lizzie's fifteen-year-old sister, Dorothea, died from lung congestion. Lizzie was never quite the same following all this. Ten years later, though, Caroline died, and it sent Lizzie over the edge.

Within a month of Caroline's death, Lizzie was exhibiting violent and unbalanced behavior and was sent to live with her parents elsewhere on the island in hopes that the change would help. She returned home after a few weeks, but she never quite recovered. On December 4, 1894, at six thirty in the evening, Lizzie called her children into the dining room for a few sips of wine, not an entirely uncommon custom in Victorian days. She had poisoned the wine, causing unbelievable suffering in the children and resulting in four of their deaths. One daughter, Wilhelmina, did not hear her mother call for them, and another, Emma, ingested the poison but recovered. Lizzie's plan was to add herself to the execution, but her plan was interrupted when her husband came into the house. A doctor was sent for but could not help. At two o'clock in the morning, following the deaths of Willie, Dora, Ella and young Lizzie, she was arrested on the charge of insanity.

Lizzie Alberti received treatment at an asylum in San Antonio and later returned to Galveston. On her return, she committed suicide and buried in the same plot as her children, an extremely rare occurrence of a murderer being buried with their own victims.

The Explosion of Rosanna Osterman

While not buried in one of Galveston's cemeteries, Rosanna Osterman is the reason for the existence of the city's first Jewish cemetery. Osterman's brother Leon was living in Texas and serving in the Revolution, one of the soldiers who escorted the captured Santa Anna in late 1836. He encouraged Rosanna's husband, Joseph, to set up a business on the island in 1837, and a year later, Rosanna followed him. They turned a small, tent-run business into a large general store and import/export operation. At that time, they were two of only thirty Jewish residents on the island. Success was great, and Joseph was able to retire by 1842, selling the business to one of his brothers-in-law, Isadore. During Rosanna's first year in Galveston, the first Jewish death occurred, that of a seven-year-old boy, who was laid to rest in the non-Jewish cemetery. Her campaign to create the first Jewish cemetery resulted in her brother Isadore donating land and the cemetery's construction in 1852. She brought in the first Jewish clergyman in Texas, Rabbi M.N. Nathan, to consecrate it.

Later, Rosanna was influential in helping those who were victims during the yellow fever outbreaks in 1853 and assisting with other epidemics between 1854 and 1866. During the Civil War, she turned her home into a hospital and possibly served as a courier of military information to Confederates in Houston. Her husband died in 1862, perishing from an accidental pistol shot. Rosanna was on board the steamboat *W.R. Carter* traveling down the Mississippi River near Vicksburg on January 30, 1866, when it exploded. She drowned in the aftermath at the age of fifty-seven. Her body was recovered afterward and buried in the Dispersed of Judah Cemetery in New Orleans. Rosanna's accumulated wealth helped establish an orphans' and widows' home in Galveston, support the Galveston Sailor's Home and the Howard Association, build synagogues in Houston and on the island and construct Jewish hospitals throughout the country.

Chapter 11

GALVESTON MEMORIAL PARK

7301 Memorial Drive
Hitchcock

Sitting along the north bank of Highland Bayou, Galveston Memorial Park is a well-maintained cemetery, residing just a block south of the much older, smaller Hitchcock Cemetery on Memorial Street. Both feature an abundance of trees and have a somewhat secluded feel to them, giving them an almost serene, park-like setting.

History

Galveston Memorial Park was organized in May 1925 by Sam Levy, Walter Norwood and Fred Pabst. The original tract was sixty-two acres, growing over the years to encompass the growth of the area. This was the first cemetery in Galveston County to offer perpetual care, and it continues to be owned and operated by Galveston County families. Many prominent families of Galveston Island and Galveston County are interred among the moss-covered oaks, magnolias and evergreen pines.

Notable Resident: Sam Maceo

Salvatore "Sam" Maceo (1894–1951) may be the most notorious figure in Galveston's history. Born in Palermo, Sicily, Maceo was a business

The grave of Sam Maceo is not inside this Maceo family mausoleum. Instead, his grave sits just to the right of this structure, hidden among the leaves and branches of the neighboring tree. *Author's collection.*

entrepreneur, power broker and racketeer who controlled for nearly thirty years not only organized crime on the island but virtually the entire government as well.

Maceo's organization, often called the Maceo Syndicate or Organization, was heavily involved in illicit and illegal activities such as gambling, prostitution, the numbers racket and bootlegging. He received substantial income from these activities, which partly benefited the island as well. Partially due to his involvement, Galveston emerged as a 1920s and 1930s nationally known open city hotspot with free-flowing liquor and vices offered in the backrooms of restaurants and nightclubs. His influence spread outside the island, throughout the state and stretched beyond, serving at times as partners to individuals like Frank Nitti and Al Capone.

By the late 1940s, corruption in Texas and Galveston County was declining and investigations into Maceo's activities ramped up. As corruption became more prevalent, plans were made to relocate to Nevada, with Sam becoming a major investor in the Desert Inn on the Las Vegas strip. Sam and his brother Rose would eventually transfer controlling interest of most of their Galveston empire to the Fertitta family before Sam's death in 1951 of cancer, just prior to the opening of the Desert Inn. Shortly thereafter, the wide-open era of Galveston ended. It took Hurricane Ike, in 2008, to take out the last remaining stronghold of Maceo's empire. The landmark Balinese Room continued to operate as a restaurant on a pier off the seawall until it was destroyed by the storm's winds and waves.

Notable Resident: B.J. Thomas

Billy Joe "B.J." Thomas (1942–2021) began singing in his church choir as a young man in Choctaw County, Oklahoma, parlaying that experience into a career. He would join the musical group the Triumphs, who in 1966 released the album *I'm So Lonesome I Could Cry*, a title Thomas would also use for a later solo album.

B.J. Thomas began his career as a choir boy in Oklahoma and later was a member of the Triumphs. However, it was as a solo act that he would make a name for himself. Two of his biggest hits were "Hooked on a Feeling" and "Raindrops Keep Fallin' on My Head," for which he won an Academy Award for Best Original Song. *Courtesy of National Archives.*

In 1968, Thomas hit the charts, making a huge impact with the release of "Hooked on a Feeling," which rose to number five in the charts. The next year, the hit movie *Butch Cassidy and the Sundance Kid* featured his song "Raindrops Keep Fallin' on My Head," which won the Academy Award for Best Original Song and obtained number one status in January 1970. More hits followed, including his second number one, "(Hey, Won't You Play) Another Somebody Done Somebody Wrong Song?"

During the mid-1970s, Thomas returned to his church choir roots, expanding his releases into gospel music from 1877 to 1981 and earning a Grammy for his recordings. While his career started to trail off during this era, he saw a resurgence when the television series *Growing Pains* used his "As Long as We Got Each Other" as its theme song for seven seasons. He continued to be an active artist, singing, writing two books and starring in two movies before revealing in March 2021 that he had been diagnosed with lung cancer. He lost that battle two months later.

Chapter 12

GLENDALE CEMETERY

8315 East Magnolia Street
Houston

Sitting atop a sloping bluff leading to the Houston Ship Channel is Houston's oldest cemetery, Glendale. This small, six-acre graveyard is cut off from the rest of the East Houston neighborhood by ship-channel businesses and a set of railroad tracks, just two blocks east of Broadway. Shading the inhabitants are numerous large live oaks and magnolia trees.

HISTORY

Established in 1826 as the Harris Family Cemetery, Glendale Cemetery predates the city of Houston by a full decade. It was one of the early sections of the new town of Harrisburg, an early city site covering nearly 4,500 acres located at the confluence of Buffalo and Bray's Bayous. While it thrived, Mexican General Antonio López de Santa Anna burned it to the ground on his way to San Jacinto, showing how important the port city was. It wasn't until 1839 that Harrisburg was rebuilt, with 1,400 people moving back, and by then the focus was on the Allen brothers' new development about a dozen miles inland.

In 1928, the growing city of Houston annexed Harrisburg. Not much remains of the once-bustling port of Harrisburg aside from the old cemetery. The cemetery itself was renamed Glendale in the 1890s. Fifteen early citizens of Texas are buried here, as are ten Civil War veterans and nearly thirty veterans of both World Wars.

Sitting on a bluff at the Houston Ship Channel is Glendale Cemetery, Houston's oldest. Small at only six acres, the cemetery is well kept, filled with numerous live oak and magnolia trees and closed to the public except for special occasions or by appointment. *Author's collection.*

LOCAL CELEBRITIES

JOHN BIRDSALL (1802–1839) was a New York politician and circuit judge who arrived in Texas in 1837. President Sam Houston appointed him the republic's attorney general shortly after his move. The next year, he was appointed by Houston to become the pro tempore chief justice of the Texas Supreme Court. Unfortunately, his term was cut short by yellow fever the following year, when he died at the age of thirty-seven. He and thirty-one others were the first to be buried in the cemetery, all victims of the epidemic and all quickly buried in a mass grave with no markers.

MARY JANE HARRIS BRISCOE (1819–1903) no longer lies resting in Glendale Cemetery; however, her presence remains. Daughter of Harris County founder John Richardson Harris and Jane Birdsall Harris, Briscoe was exhumed and moved to Glenwood Cemetery, although a stone remains and is maintained at Glendale. She became the wife of Andrew W. Briscoe (buried in Austin's State Cemetery), who was a signer of the Texas Declaration of Independence and a captain of the regulars at San Jacinto. She also founded the Daughters of the Republic of Texas.

Notable Resident: Jane Birdsall Harris

Jane Birdsall Harris (1791–1869) was an innkeeper and hostess to the republic's provisional government in Harrisburg. Married to John R. Harris in New York, she moved with her husband and their four children to Missouri, remaining until 1824 before returning to New York with the children while John prepared for them to settle in Texas. They remained there until 1833, when Jane moved to Harrisburg, Texas, four years after her husband's death.

In Harrisburg, during March and April 1836, Jane hosted the provisional government in her home. It was so crowded that nearly everyone had to sleep on the floor—save the president, vice president and secretary of state. During the Runaway Scrape, she fled Harrisburg, first to Anahuac and then Galveston. Following the Battle of San Jacinto she returned, building a new dwelling, with labor provided by Mexican prisoners of war, to replace the one destroyed by the pursuant Mexican army. She would continue to be involved in the growth of Harrisburg, serving as a stockholder in the town company and operating a popular inn until her 1869 death.

Notable Resident: John Grant Tod Sr.

Naval officer John Grant Tod Sr. (1808–1877) was one of the founders of the first railroad in Texas. After leaving home at seventeen, he traveled down the Mississippi River from his home in Kentucky to New Orleans, where he joined the Mexican navy. Later he was commissioned a midshipman in the U.S. Navy, served briefly as a customs inspector at Velasco, was appointed a naval inspector in 1838 at the Galveston naval station, served as one of the Texas navy's purchasing agents in Baltimore and, in July 1839, was appointed a commander in the navy, placed in command the following year of the naval station at Galveston before serving as acting secretary of the navy. He would later resign his post over faltering navy finances and act as a lobbyist for the republic, where he lobbied for annexation. In 1845, he returned from Washington to Texas, carrying the official notification of annexation.

Tod would return to the military, serving during the Mexican War in the U.S. navy and as an agent of the quartermaster general at the Brazos Santiago Depot and at New Orleans. After resigning from the service in

1847, he put his efforts into the need for railroads in Texas, eventually helping found the Buffalo Bayou, Brazos and Colorado Railway. His other interests included the construction of the Galveston customhouse and post office and developing several businesses in Galveston County.

Chapter 13

GLENWOOD CEMETERY

2525 Washington Avenue
Houston

Located on two tracts of land on the north side of Buffalo Bayou and west of downtown Houston, Glenwood Cemetery is the pinnacle resting place of Houston's elite citizenry and is widely known as the River Oaks of the Dead. While there is a back entrance to the cemetery grounds off Sawyer Street at Kane Street, the primary way to visit is through the wooded, landscaped and gated entrance off Washington Avenue. On the grounds, visitors will find numerous hardwoods and bluffs cut by deep ravines leading toward the bayou.

Parts of the property still afford great views of Houston's downtown skyline, Memorial Drive and Allen Parkway. Additionally, the cemetery's horticultural specimens could rival those of many arboretums, the collection of Victorian statuary is worthy of an art museum and the large expanse of land, a quiet refuge among the skyscrapers, provides a place for peaceful reflection and meditation.

History

The land on which Glenwood sits was once the country estate and brickyard of William Harrison King, a onetime Houston mayor. It sat well outside of Houston and was established in a rural area. When Alfred Whitaker chartered the Houston Cemetery Company, he purchased this property along with some adjacent land in 1870. Whitaker's landscaping company cleared the lots, laid out and graded rights-of-way and generally beautified the land. In June 1872, Glenwood opened as the city's first professionally designed cemetery; newspaper accounts at the time compared it to garden cemetery parks like Philadelphia's Lauren Hill and Green-Wood in Brooklyn.

Over the years, new sections were developed, infrastructure was constructed and improvements continued, including the addition of a conservatory/greenhouse and the superintendent's residence and the installation of an irrigation system and fountains. By 1874, Glenwood had become a recreational destination and, throughout the 1880s and '90s, continued to serve as an entertainment attraction. A mule-drawn street railway operated on Washington Road, shuttling people to the cemetery for weekend and holiday visits. Following a brief period of neglect, revitalization came again in the early twentieth century. A masonry bridge crossing was added to the entrance to replace the irreparable original wood one; brick and masonry gateposts and ornamental iron fencing and gates were added around 1900; and the beautification of the lake, the addition of retaining walls and a levee and significant drainage work was all undertaken.

Since that time, Glenwood has continued to improve. In 1925, the shell gravel roads were paved and the cemetery had to deal with Buffalo Bayou's rechanneling and the construction of Memorial Drive. The office cottage has been improved and expanded, a belvedere added and the guardhouse constructed near the entrance bridge. In 1999, the adjacent Washington Cemetery was acquired. Today, the Glenwood Cemetery Historic Preservation Foundation oversees the historic preservation aspect of the property along with the scope of day-to-day maintenance and operation. The first of three roads connecting the two cemeteries was added in 2000. More recently, Glenwood closed its main entrance to continue improvement and to add a visitor's center.

Memorable Headstones

Ogham Stone Headstone

The Ogham stone, inscribed with a series of Celtic strokes, marks the grave site of Barbara and Marks Hinton. Ogham stones are inscribed with personal names and commemorations, and the alphabet consists of a series of strokes. Here, the last name "Hinton" is read from the bottom of the stone to the top.

In a cemetery of unique headstones and markers lies the Ogham stone. Inscribed with a series of Celtic strokes, the stone is short hike up from the road and marks the grave of Barbara and Marks Hinton. *Author's collection.*

Fireman's Memorial: Died in the Line of Duty

Honoring the Houston firefighters who gave their lives in the line of duty, this monument is topped by a life-size statue. Prior to the beginning of the paid department, Houston's fire protection came from several volunteer fire companies. In 1888, they banded together and bought a plot in Glenwood Cemetery to be used for members of the department. That June, they ordered this memorial, topped with the likeness of Robert Brewster, the oldest living member at that time. Eight firefighters were buried there. Nearly ninety years later, in 1976, the fire department moved the monument to its headquarters before returning it to its original location in the early 1990s. Memorials continued to be held there until the new Firefighters Pension Office and Memorial Gardens opened north of the city in 2001. Nearby is the grave site of Anne McCormick Sullivan (1988–2013). She died in the line of duty battling the May 31, 2013 five-alarm Southwest Motel fire that also killed four other firefighters. It was the single worst loss of life in the department's history.

Eliza Allen Converse

It is said that Eliza Converse (1838–1886), daughter of Augustus Chapman Allen, was the first child to be born in the city of Houston.

The Angel of Grief

The Angel of Grief statue, long used for photographs and to showcase the cemetery's rich artistic designs, depicts a winged angel draped over the base of a headstone; this design is one of the most copied images in the world. Originally, it was sculpted in 1894 by William Wetmore Story for the grave of his wife, Emelyn, at the Protestant Cemetery in Rome. In Houston, it adorns the Hill Monument. Glenwood's angel is one of five of its kind that can be found in Texas and was sculpted by Frank Teich, a German sculptor and stonecutter, who also created the Sam Houston monument in Houston's Hermann Park.

Right: Fronted by a handful of firefighters who have died in the line of duty is the Fireman's Memorial. The monument is topped with a statue of Robert Brewster, the oldest living member of the Houston Fire Service at that time. *Author's collection.*

Below: The Angel of Grief is a well known and often photographed statue in Glenwood. This design comes from an artist who placed it at his wife's grave in Rome. This statue is one of five of its kind that can be found in Texas and was sculpted by German artist Frank Teich. *Author's collection.*

Local Celebrities

Colonel Walter Browne Botts (1835–1894), a lawyer and Confederate infantry officer, migrated to Houston in 1857, entering a law practice with Peter Gray. He enlisted in the Fifth Texas Infantry in 1861 and was later promoted to major and then lieutenant colonel, seeing action at all major campaigns of the Army of Northern Virginia and later at Suffolk, Knoxville and Chickamauga. Botts resigned after an illness and hospital stay and then returned to Texas, where he resumed his law practice, which evolved into one of the most well-known law firms in Texas, Baker and Botts.

Edward M. House (1858–1938) was an influential "behind-the-scenes" politician who helped four successive governors win their office in Texas; James Hogg, the first, bestowed on him his honorary title of colonel. He is best known as a diplomat who served as the chief advisor to President Woodrow Wilson, becoming influential in his campaign for president (and, later, reelection) and transitioning to become his most trusted advisor, choosing to remain outside of any cabinet positions. He played a major role in negotiating wartime democracy, negotiated acceptance of Wilson's Fourteen Points as a basis for a peace treaty to end World War I and then served as a member of the U.S. delegation to the Paris Peace Conference in 1919. He also worked closely with Wilson to draft the covenant of the League of Nations, advocating for the independence of Poland, where he is considered a hero; there is a statue of him in Skaryszewski Park in Warsaw.

William Stamps Farish II (1881–1942), an oil field pioneer, provided $1 million capital for Humble Oil (now part of ExxonMobil) to be incorporated, became president of Standard Oil (later Exxon) and built one of the world's largest refineries in Baytown. Appointed by John D. Rockefeller to serve as chairman of Standard Oil, he later became its president and a founder of the American Petroleum Institute.

Florence Sterling (1871–1940) was an early women's rights activist in Texas. Born in Anahuac as one of twelve children, she worked with her brothers in her father's store and then at R.S. Sterling & Co. as a bookkeeper and as secretary and treasurer and, later, full treasurer and secretary of the Humble Oil Company, hiding her gender by signing business checks as F.S. Sterling.

During World War I, Sterling was a member of the executive board of the Houston Red Cross and worked as a treasurer of the Houston War Camp

Community Service. She served as a vice president of the Texas branch of the National Woman's Party, was involved in the Texas branch of the Congressional Union for Women's Suffrage, served as the president of the League of Women Voters in Houston and founded, in 1923, *Women's Viewpoint*, a publication edited and written entirely by women until 1927.

ANNETTE FINNIGAN (1873–1940) was raised in Houston before her family moved to New York City, where her father oversaw his successful John Finnigan Hide Company business. Back East, she studied at Wellesley and Columbia and then found employment in the family business. When the family returned to Houston, they became founding members of the Houston Equal Suffrage League, and Annette's efforts continued in the movement until her death. Along the way, she assumed control of her father's estate, running the John Finnigan Hide Company, the Houston Packing Company and the Hotel Brazos Company following his death. She led the push to pass an amendment to give women the right to vote, working with the Women's Political Union and the Texas Women's Suffrage Association. Her philanthropic efforts also helped establish the Houston Public Library and added hundreds of objects to the Museum of Fine Arts, Houston.

JAMES ADDISON BAKER JR. (1857–1941), Houston attorney and banker, went by "Captain Baker" for most of his life, signing his name as such following the 1897 death of his father. As a young attorney, Baker specialized in railroad law, beneficial as the city was growing into a regional transportation hub. Through this, he developed a business relationship with William Marsh Rice, serving first as his attorney and later overseeing Rice's business interests in a multitude of companies. He defended his client's estate against a will probated under Rice's second wife's signature and then unraveled a murder conspiracy in New York that was executed by Rice's personal valet and another attorney. His evidence led to their convictions in what was the "crime of the century" at the time.

Baker would continue to serve as a trustee for the Rice Institute for another five decades. Additionally, he worked for a variety of clients, especially in Houston's robust early oil and gas industry. He served as the president of the Houston Bar Association, the Houston Gas Company and the Guardian Trust Company and helped organize the Southwestern Drug Company and the Galveston, Houston and Henderson Railway. He was also instrumental in helping organize and lead banks through the financial crisis following the 1929 Wall Street crash.

At sixty-four feet tall and with a trunk as wide as a Volkswagen, this cemetery oak makes a huge statement in Glenwood. Located in the Forest Mound section, where the graves date to the 1910s, this tree is evidence of a time when Glenwood served Houston not only as a burial ground but also as a park to visit for leisure. *Author's collection.*

The designs of architect EUGENE HEINER (1852–1901) pepper the landscape of Texas. Born in New York City, he apprenticed in Chicago and Germany before moving to Dallas in 1977, relocating to Houston the following year. In Houston, he established a practice that would last the rest of his career. One of his first designs was awarded through a design competition, earning him a commission to design the Galveston County Jailhouse. In addition to numerous Texas jails over the next two decades, he designed courthouses (those in Colorado, Lavaca and Brazoria Counties are on the National Register of Historic Places) and is credited with the design of buildings on the campuses of Texas A&M in College Station and at the Texas State Penitentiary at Huntsville. Some of the best-known historic buildings in downtown Houston were designed by him and include the Houston Cotton Exchange, the W.L. Foley Building and the Sweeney and Coombs Opera House.

MARGARET KINKAID (1874–1951), elementary teacher at Houston's Hawthorne Elementary, received a rude awakening following her marriage to William J. Kinkaid in 1899. Married women were not allowed to teach in the Houston public school system. Rather than give up her profession, she invited seven students to begin classes in her home in September 1904. A brief interruption came when she gave birth to her second son in 1906 before resuming classes, later citing that date as the beginning of the Kinkaid School. The school had outgrown her home by the 1920s, and she worked with a board of some of Houston's most influential men to raise funds for a new permanent and enlarged school. The school prospered and grew under her leadership and that of her son William, who would serve as the principal from 1941 to 1951. Margaret retired in 1951, shortly before dying in an automobile accident that December.

Agnese Carter Nelms (1889–1967) was a pioneer in the birth control movement in Texas. Nelms helped open River Oaks Elementary School and led a major push for the creation of birth control clinics in Houston. She helped finance and staff services and clinics for women regardless of race or means and raised awareness of what was considered a taboo topic, despite facing public scorn.

Architect John Staub (1892–1981) was a longtime Houston residential architect, with works spanning from 1921 to 1963. Originally brought to Houston on assignment for the Shadyside subdivision, Staub decided to stay and open his own firm. His work includes the River Oaks Country Club, Ima Hogg's mansion at Bayou Bend and numerous homes in Broadacres, Cortland Place and River Oaks. He also designed landmarks such as the Junior League Building, the Bayou Club and multiple buildings at Rice University, University of Houston and in the Texas Medical center.

Lumberman Samuel Fain Carter (1857–1928) worked in the newspaper business in Sherman and at Galveston as a young man before entering the lumber business in Beaumont as a bookkeeper. Carter was so adept with the industry that he was placed managing a sawmill plant and then became manager of the entire business in Beaumont. He moved to Houston in 1892 and organized his own company, the Lumberman's National Bank, and served as president or director of several other Houston businesses.

Former American Cotton Company assistant general manager Will Clayton (1880 –1966) moved his operations from Oklahoma to Houston in 1916. Clayton led other cotton exporters in providing warehouse facilities, insurance, credit and other services that European firms had formerly supplied, bringing operations into Latin America and Africa. Carter fought New Deal policies, wanting support to go directly to farmers rather than the agricultural market. He served on committees and boards that were crucial to wartime efforts in both World Wars and was a principal architect of the European Recovery Program, known commonly as the Marshall Plan.

EDNA DEE WOOLFORD SAUNDERS (1880–1963) almost single-handedly transformed Houston's cultural landscape into a national center. Eschewing her extensive voice and piano training, Saunders chose instead to bring the arts to the people of Houston. Saunders would book events for Houston's City Auditorium in a career spanning forty-five years. Acts and ensembles included Enrico Caruso, Sergei Rachmaninoff, Ernestine Schumann-Heink, the New York Philharmonic Orchestra, the St. Louis Symphony Orchestra, the acclaimed Ballet Russe de Monte Carlo, the National Ballet of Canada and the American Ballet Theatre, with big-name performers brought in to help offset low-revenue classical programming, such as Will Rogers, Katharine Hepburn and Bob Hope. For Marian Anderson's first concert, Saunders got city approval to shift seating arrangements in the City Auditorium, moving the traditional "Blacks only" section from the balcony to the main floor and dividing the floor to seat Blacks on one side and Whites on the other; she and the Houston mayor sat with civic leaders of the African American community on the Black side of the floor.

NOTABLE RESIDENT: DANIEL DENTON COOLEY

Known as the Father of Houston Heights, Daniel Denton Cooley (1850–1933) settled in Ashland, Nebraska, as a young man, working in the mercantile business and as a cashier for the First National Bank. In 1887, bank president Oscar Martin Carter formed the Omaha and South Texas Land Company, a subsidiary of the American Loan and Trust Company, and appointed Cooley its director, treasurer and general manager.

In May 1891, the company purchased over 1,700 acres of land just west of downtown Houston and twenty feet higher in elevation, leading to its name. At the time, Houston Heights was one of the largest real estate projects in the country. Cooley's house was one of the division's first, and he installed electric lights in the home by hooking wires from the house to the nearby electric trolley line. Cooley played a key role in laying out the new community's streets in establishing the Cooley School, served as an alderman and helped build the Jefferson Davis County Hospital, St. Andrew's Church and St. Stephen's Mission. He also was involved in fraternal organizations, the South Texas National Bank, the Houston Electric Company and the Electric Street Railway Company and was president of the State Land Oil Company (now merged with Gulf Oil) and the Houston Railway Company.

Notable Resident: Roy Hofheinz

Known better as Judge Hofheinz or the Judge, Roy Hofheinz (1912–1982) served as a Texas state representative, county judge of Harris County and mayor of Houston. His legacy is as the father of the Astrodome. His public elected life was tumultuous and included an impeachment; when he returned to private practice and business, he created the Houston Sports Association (HSA), which evolved into several ventures. Despite heavy criticism for its plan to build a giant roofed sports stadium, HSA received an MLB franchise under that promise, and in 1965, the world's first domed stadium was completed. Hofheinz claimed the Astrodome was the "Eighth Wonder of the World." It would become home to the Houston Colt .45s/Astros, the NFL Oilers, the Houston Rodeo and Livestock Show and numerous special events. Adjacent to the Astrodome, Hofheinz developed the South Loop, adding the Astroworld amusement park, the Ringling Brothers and Barnum and Bailey Circus and four Astrodomain hotels. After a stroke, Hofheinz's businesses suffered, and he sold off his interests in these once-lucrative ventures. He died of a heart attack at his home in Houston on November 22, 1982.

Notable Residents: William P. and Oveta Culp Hobby

William P. Hobby (1878–1964), already a well-known publisher, served as the youngest governor of Texas at age thirty-nine, setting up a statewide military draft for World War I and passing measures regarding state aid, oil and gas and education. After losing reelection in 1924, he was elected president of the *Houston Post* and later, as chairman of that company, acquired radio and television stations, including KPRC. The international airport downtown was named for him in 1967.

The Hobbys, William and Oveta, were one of Houston's early power couples. Hobby served as the youngest governor of Texas at the age of thirty-nine, was a well-known publisher and acquired radio and television stations. Oveta may have been the more accomplished of the two, involved in newspapers and World War II and becoming the first secretary of the Department of Health, Education and Welfare—the only woman to serve in Eisenhower's cabinet. *Author's collection.*

His wife, Oveta Culp Hobby (1905–1995), was just as accomplished, if not more so. She served as manager of the *Houston Post*, one of the nation's leading newspapers; served as parliamentarian for the Texas House of Representatives; organized the Women's Auxiliary Army Corps (WAAC) during World War II; and became America's first female colonel, receiving the Distinguished Service Medal in 1945 for her service. She also served on the boards of numerous organizations—Rice University, the Corporation for Public Broadcasting; the Museum of Fine Arts, Houston; and the American National Red Cross, among others—and was a member of the U.S. delegation to the UN Conference on Freedom of Information and the Press in Geneva. As the first secretary of the Department of Health, Education and Welfare, she pioneered the role, the only woman to serve in President Eisenhower's cabinet.

Notable Resident: Ross S. Sterling

Ross Sterling (1875–1949) was cofounder of the Humble Oil Company (now part of ExxonMobil) with his siblings Frank and Florence Sterling and other prominent oilmen Harry Weiss and R.L. Blaffer. Also involved in the railroad industry and the newspaper business, buying both the *Houston Post* and the *Houston Dispatch*, combining them to be the *Houston Post-Dispatch* before dropping the "Dispatch" part of the name. Sterling would serve as the thirty-first governor of Texas for one term in 1931–32. Following that, he served as president of the Sterling Oil and Refining Co., American Maid Flour Mills and R.S. Sterling Investment Company and as chairman of the Houston National Bank and Houston-Harris County Channel Navigation Board. His mansion, in La Porte, was designed to look like the White House and still stands.

Notable Resident: George Hermann

The last name of George Hermann (1843–1914) is hung on many spaces throughout Houston, such as Hermann Hospital, Hermann Park and Hermann Square at city hall. He came from humble beginnings, lived very frugally and amassed a great fortune, which he would later find great joy in bestowing as gifts to the city. After serving in the Civil War, he got involved in the cattle business and dealt in real estate, striking it rich when his tract of land was at the center of the big Humble oil field. He donated hundreds of acres to support the establishment of sites such as a charitable hospital, Hermann Park (the site of the Houston Zoo today) and a small parcel in front of city hall, the site of his childhood home. He also donated land to the Houston Art League for a public museum, now the Museum of Fine Arts, Houston. When he donated the land for Hermann Park, he said that that was the happiest day of his life.

Notable Resident: Glenn McCarthy

Known as the Legendary King of the Wildcatters, Glenn McCarthy (1907–1988) began in the oil fields at the age of eight as a water boy. Throughout

Gene Tierney fled her privileged and wealthy upbringing for the lights of Broadway and then Hollywood. She starred in numerous films, but it was Alfred Hitchcock's *Laura* that made her a major star. She remarried in 1960 to W. Howard Lee, an oil executive (who is also laid to rest here) and Hedy Lamarr's ex-husband. *Author's collection.*

his life, he would strike oil thirty-eight times and discover eleven Texas oil fields. McCarthy built the Shamrock Hotel and owned numerous ventures, including several oil and gas companies, KXYZ Radio, fourteen newspapers, a magazine, a movie production company, the Shell buildings and two banks. He was friends with the likes of John Wayne and Howard Hughes and is considered the model for the character of Jett Rink in Edna Ferber's book *Giant*.

Notable Resident: Gene Tierney Lee

New York native Gene Tierney (1920–1991) enjoyed a privileged and wealthy upbringing that included private schools and finishing school in Switzerland. Afterward, she had an interest in acting and pursued the craft on Broadway. In the early 1940s, she relocated to Hollywood, establishing herself as a star for 20th Century Fox in films such as *The Return of Frank James*, *Belle Starr* and *Heaven Can Wait*. Her 1944 portrayal of the titular character *Laura* made her a major screen star, and she was nominated for an Oscar two years later for her role in *Leave Her to Heaven*. In her marriage to designer Oleg Cassini, she gave birth to a severely brain-damaged daughter and had another in 1948; the couple divorced four years later. She continued acting in films such as *The Razor's Edge*, *The Ghost and Mrs. Muir* and *The Left Hand of God*. In 1955, she left Hollywood due to stress and depression and admitted herself to the Menninger Clinic in Topeka, Kansas. Determined to regain a happy life, she remarried in 1960 to oil executive (and former husband to Hedy Lamarr) W. Howard Lee. Tierney acted in a few more movies in the 1960s but had joined her new husband in Houston and eventually retired from films, acting in only a few television appearances over the years. Instead, she traveled with her husband and participated in civic and charitable causes. She died of emphysema in Houston in 1991.

Notable Resident: Howard Hughes Sr.

Howard Hughes Sr. (1869–1924) would become best known as the father and namesake of the famous business tycoon; however, he made a strong impact on the American landscape himself. He engaged in various mining endeavors but found luck capitalizing on the Spindletop oil discovery near

The Hughes family is buried at this monumental promenade. Both the wunderkind Howard Hughes Jr. and his father, the pioneering tool inventor, are buried in the family plot. Hughes Sr. made the family name famous in Houston, while his son took it to new heights with his activities. *Author's collection.*

Beaumont, devoting all his effort toward that, much of it with early business partner Walter B. Sharp. In 1908, he filed the basic patents for the Sharp-Hughes Rock Bit, a two-cone rotary drill bit that could penetrate medium and hard rock with ten times the speed of any competitor. The following year, he and Sharp founded the Sharp-Hughes Tool Company.

Following his death in 1924 inside the company's offices on the fifth floor of the Humble Oil building in Houston, his only child, nineteen-year-old Howard Jr., assumed control as primary owner of the company. The following year, Howard Jr. had himself declared an adult and bought out his remaining family in the business to control the entirety of Hughes Tool Company.

Notable Resident: Howard Hughes Jr.

Born in Houston, Howard Hughes Jr. (1905–1976) was thrust into wealth and power at an early age. Following his father's death, he assumed control of the Hughes Tool Company at age nineteen and, along with it, an estate of nearly $1 million. He moved to Hollywood in the late 1920s, where he produced *Hell's Angels*, *The Outlaw* and *Scarface*. He also earned an Academy Award for best comedy direction for *Two Arabian Nights*. During World War II and following, he pursued an interest in aviation, forming Hughes Aviation and piloting one of his airplanes to a new world speed record, and became a major aerospace and defense contractor, receiving government contracts for development and manufacture of aircraft. While his flying wooden boat, dubbed the Spruce Goose, failed, in 1956, he acquired Trans World Airlines (TWA) and pushed aviation into the jet age.

By the late 1960s, he was sliding into reclusiveness and eventually began running his business from a Desert Inn penthouse in Las Vegas. By the 1970s, he was the largest single landholder in Nevada and the state's largest employer, with around eight thousand residents on his payroll. He spent the final years of his life flitting between hotels in London, Nicaragua, Vancouver, the Bahamas and Acapulco, where he was traveling from to Houston when he died. Additionally, he created the Howard Hughes Medical Institution in late 1953. It was infused with the profits of his aircraft company and its sale after his death, and it continues to be a leading biological and medical research institute and runs the largest privately funded education initiative in the United States.

NOTABLE RESIDENT: WILLIAM WARD WATKIN

William Ward Watkin (1886–1952) came to Houston in 1910 to oversee the construction of Rice Institute for the Boston firm of Cram, Goodhue and Ferguson and decided to stay. He was appointed by Edgar Odell Lovett to head Rice's architecture department and established a prolific practice that included the design of the original Museum of Fine Arts, Houston building. Watkin also designed many educational institutions and was a specialist in church architecture, building several chapels and churches in Houston, including Trinity Episcopal Church. He also designed a home for the family of Howard Hughes and was responsible for Broadacres' oak alleles and other design features and the Hughes family grave sites at Glenwood.

NOTABLE RESIDENT: DR. DENTON A. COOLEY

Dr. Denton A. Cooley (1920–2016) was a cardiothoracic surgeon most famously known for performing the first total artificial heart transplant in 1969. The transplant also led to a forty-year feud with his mentor and partner Dr. DeBakey. Cooley also performed the first heart transplant in the United States in 1968 and the first lung and heart transplant, to the same patient, in 1969 and pioneered countless heart and blood vessel surgical techniques, including one that reduced the need for blood transfusions in open-heart operations. He received the highest award a civilian can receive, the Presidential Medal of Freedom, in 1984. Cooley was also the founder and surgeon-in-chief of the Texas Heart Institute at St. Luke's Hospital and chief of cardiovascular surgery at Baylor St. Luke's Medical Center and was involved with Texas Children's Hospital and the University of Texas Health Science Center at Houston.

The grave of Dr. Denton Cooley is marked by a large stone heart. The famous cardiothoracic surgeon is famous for having performed the first total artificial heart transplant in 1969, here in Houston. *Author's collection.*

Notable Resident: Rufus Daniels

Rufus Daniels (1861–1917), along with officers Ira Raney, Daniel Patton, Horace Moody and Edward Meinecke, was shot and killed during the Camp Logan Riot. He had served the Houston Police Department (HPD) for six years when he died at age fifty-six, leaving behind a wife and two children. Around noon on August 23, 1917, along with officer Lee Sparks, he disrupted a gathering on a street corner in the San Felipe district (a predominately Black Houston district) by firing warning shots. The officers pursued those who fled, bursting into the home of Sara Travers, who was dragged outside and arrested. The violence between the men of Camp Logan and Officers Sparks and Daniels escalated throughout the day until Corporal Charles Baltimore approached the officers later in the afternoon to inquire about Edwards and was hit with a pistol by Sparks. He fled and was pulled out of a home, beaten and placed under arrest, but the rumor was that he had been killed—a rumor that made it back to camp. At this point, the men of the camp decided they'd had enough and plotted to mutiny, riot and exact revenge. Baltimore's subsequent release and return to Camp Logan alive did nothing to quell the impending riot. HPD responded in a disorganized fashion, partially believing the soldiers would be unable to arm themselves, and only a small number of officers were sent out, expecting a quick squashing of the uprising. The first police casualties occurred when a group of six officers stumbled on the large numbers of armed soldiers. Two policemen, including Daniels, were killed immediately, and one later died of wounds. His grave site had no marker until 2006, when the 100 Club of Houston-Harris County placed a "Killed in the Line of Duty" marker on his grave site in the Flower Mound section of Glenwood.

Notable Resident: Anson Jones

Physician Anson Jones (1798–1858) served as the final president of the Republic of Texas. When annexation occurred in 1846, Jones gave an eloquent speech at the capitol in Austin expressing hopes for a happy and perpetual union with the United States. Afterward, he and Sam Houston lowered the flag of the republic and raised the Stars and Stripes. During

Jones's administration, he led efforts that would result in a university system for higher education. After annexation, he was defeated in several legislative office bids and was thrown from a horse in 1849, sustaining several injuries. Brooding over his career during a stay at Houston's old Capitol Hotel in 1858, Jones returned to his room and fatally shot himself.

Notable Resident: Colonel Benjamin Franklin Terry

Colonel B.F. Terry (1821–1861) had already made a name for himself by the time the Civil War rolled into town. He helped construct the first railroad in Texas (the Buffalo Bayou, Brazos and Colorado Railway) and purchased the Oakland sugar plantations in Fort Bend County in 1852, becoming a prosperous sugar planter. His popularity and wealth landed him a delegate spot at the Secession Convention, which led to him later volunteering his services to the Confederate army. He would organize and command the Eighth Texas Cavalry regiment as Terry's Texas Rangers. He was killed in the first battle fought by the regiment in Woodsonville, Kentucky, in 1861.

Notable Resident: Charlotte Baldwin Allen

Hailed as the "mother of Houston," Charlotte Baldwin Allen (1805–1895) was the wife of Augustus Chapman Allen, and the founding of the city revolved around her doorstep. The year following their marriage, Augustus, along with his brother John Kirby, came to Texas. They settled first in San Augustine and then at Nacogdoches, with Charlotte arriving in 1834.

Through her inheritance, the brothers purchased half a league of land on Buffalo Bayou in August 1836 at the price of $5,000. Four days later, they advertised the establishment of a new city, Houston—the name may have been Charlotte's suggestion. The new settlement was quickly settled and became the capital of the nascent republic from 1837 to 1839. Near their home at Prairie and Caroline, the brothers built the first statehouse, and Sam Houston lived next door to the couple. When John Allen died in 1838, the couple disagreed over the estate settlement, leading to their separation in 1850. Augustus moved on, first to Mexico and then to Washington, D.C. Where he died in 1864, Charlotte remained in Houston, where she watched the city grow up around her. On her passing, she deeded property to the city to locate a city hall and market house, an area now called Market Square.

Eerie Tales: Leona Tonn

Legend has it that the graveyard's former owner, Leona Tonn, a murder victim, haunts the grounds. Glenwood is adjoined with Washington Cemetery, which Leona looked after until her 1977 murder—a murder that remains unsolved to this day. The cemetery was financially abandoned in the mid-twentieth century. Leona, the caretaker's widow, attempted to keep up with the work until she died. Afterward, the graveyard was severely neglected. Leona lived in a house on the property and was found by her brother with a pillowcase tied over her head, suffocated to death. The murder is unsolved.

Chapter 14

HODGE'S BEND CEMETERY

17245 Old Richmond Road
Sugar Land

Located along a bend on the Old Richmond Road in Fort Bend, Hodge's Bend Cemetery appears to be slightly more than a quick drive-by. Nested with giant trees and nearby forested growth, this cemetery is a beautifully simple old graveyard. It lies opposite the Pheasant Creek subdivision, along the bank of White Lake.

History

This cemetery sits on Hodge's Bend, part of Alexander Hodge's 1828 land grant from Stephan F. Austin. Burials began early, the first being that of Alexander's wife, Ruth, who died in 1831 and was buried here in 1836. The final burial to take place on the land was that of Mattie White, in 1942. In between, roughly seventy others were laid to rest here. For around 150 years, the Columbia Bottomland of Hodge's property was used to raise cattle, sugarcane and other crops. Since then, the City of Sugarland has developed part of Hodge's land, including the adjacent Cullinan Park, to which the cemetery is connected through a series of pathways.

Notable Resident: Alexander Hodge

Alexander Hodge has one of the oldest marked headstones in the area. At the age of fourteen, future Fort Bend resident Hodge would join "Swamp Fox" Francis Marion's South Carolina Brigade and fight for the nascent United States during the American Revolution. *Author's collection.*

Alexander Hodge (1757–1836) brought his family to Texas in 1825. He had previously served in the American Revolution. At the age of fourteen, Hodge would join "Swamp Fox" Francis Marion's South Carolina Brigade. Following the Revolution, Hodge migrated westward, landing first in Kentucky and then Arkansas. There he met Stephen F. Austin, who convinced Hodge to continue to Texas with his family, offering him one of his personal leagues of land along the Brazos River; he would name it Hodge's Bend.

Hodge was prominent among Stephen F. Austin's Old Three Hundred settlers. While Hodge himself did not fight during the Texas Revolution, his sons did, and he belonged to the Texas militia and gathered his family to stay ahead of the fighting as it headed eastward. Of the many veterans of the American Revolution who migrated westward, only fifty are known to be buried in Texas and only one, Hodge, is known to be buried in Fort Bend County.

Special Features

Jaybird-Woodpecker War Monument

This monument to the Jaybird-Woodpecker War once stood on the grounds next to Richmond's city hall. It is known as the "Our Heroes" statue, and calls for a move of the statue, which represents a racially motivated part of Fort Bend County's history, came in 2020.

The war was a feud between two political factions for control of the county. The Jaybirds represented wealth and roughly 90 percent of the White population. The Woodpeckers, about forty people, were current and former officials who held office because of the Black vote for the Republican ticket. Both parties claimed to be Democrats, but it was the Jaybirds who sought to rid the county of the Republican government that had gained control during

Among the headstones of Hodge's Bend lies a monument to the Jaybird-Woodpecker War. Fought along the grounds of Richmond's City Hall, the battle was a feud between two political factions for control of the county and based almost entirely on racial strife. After calls for the statue's removal from the city hall grounds, it was placed at Hodge's Bend. *Author's collection.*

Reconstruction. Tensions boiled over during the 1888 elections, leading to violent altercations between rival candidates. One Jaybird leader was killed, and others were wounded in various interactions.

At one Jaybird mass meeting in September, attendees resolved to warn certain Black people to leave the county within ten hours. Members of both factions were armed. The Texas Rangers were stationed in Richmond, and there was a heavy voter turnout on election day, which eventually passed peacefully. The gap between the factions widened afterward, though, with insults, threats and assaults leading to more killings and turning the county into an armed camp, eventually leading to the Battle of Richmond on August 16, 1889.

The battle took place primarily around the courthouse and the downtown district. The Jaybirds would result triumphant, but casualties were heavy. The Houston Light Guards arrived to establish martial law, and Governor Lawrence S. Ross and the Brenham Light Guards arrived shortly thereafter, with Governor Ross remaining for several days to mediate the situation. The result was the removal or resignation of all Woodpecker officials and the selection of either Jaybirds, or Jaybird-friendly people, to fill the offices, giving control of the government back to the White citizenry through the establishment of the Jaybird Democratic Organization of Fort Bend County. This organization played a dominant role in county politics for the next seven decades, and its influence still flows through the county. The statue was erected to honor three Jaybird members who were killed in the shootout battle.

Chapter 15

HOLLYWOOD CEMETERY

3506 North Main Street
Houston

Situated off the hectic off-ramps of I-45 and just north of downtown, Hollywood Cemetery's sprawling, rolling landscape belies its location. While headstones and memorials are packed rather tightly throughout, they are still only slightly scattered at the fringes of the cemetery's property, showcasing its current usage as an active cemetery.

HISTORY

Hollywood Cemetery was founded by brothers Williams James and Samuel B. Moore in 1895; the two Confederate veterans made several land deals to purchase the fifty-five-acre site. The cemetery got its name from the Hollywood family, admired by one of the brothers and eventually laid to rest in their namesake burial ground. The original main entryway to Hollywood was near the Trimble and Cottage Streets intersection, northwest of its present location, crossing over a single-lane bridge at Little White Oak Bayou. The original brick road through the cemetery remains but has been paved over in recent years.

Following several years of poor management, the property went into foreclosure and was eventually purchased in 2009. It was renamed Historic Hollywood Cemetery and received a Texas Register of Historic Places marker. By the 2010s, Hollywood could count over thirty thousand interments.

Local Celebrities

In 1936, Lawrence Shipley Sr. (1906–1997) developed a unique recipe that would change the breakfast market in Houston. Using a mix of whole wheat and potato flour, Shipley found a way to make a delicious doughnut that was substantially less greasy than his competitors'. At the start, Shipley sold them only wholesale at a nickel per dozen. However, by the 1940s, the Shipley family had entered the retail business with stores opening in Houston, first at 1417 Crockett Street. Lawrence's wife, Lillie Shipley (1912–2002; buried next to him), ran the retail side of the operation. Later, their son, Lawrence "Bud" Jr. (1936–2005; also buried in this cemetery), joined the business and expanded operations by adding 190 stores throughout Texas, Alabama, Arkansas, Louisiana, Mississippi and Tennessee (Colorado, Oklahoma and Florida have been added since, through a franchise system that now numbers over three hundred stores). Shipley's offers over sixty varieties of doughnuts, although Lawrence's original plain glazed remains its top seller.

Sarah Jane Gillis (1826–1938) is likely one of the oldest persons to have lived in Houston, dying at a reputed 111 years old. Born on Christmas, at nine years old she hid in the brush near her home along Buffalo Bayou, at Harrisburg, when General Santa Anna came through and burned the family home. Her father fought in the ensuing Battle of San Jacinto. She married three times, living in Grimes County, in New Orleans, on the Beaumont Road and lastly at Humble. Having no money for a headstone, she was buried in an unmarked grave in a plot owned by good friends, between the Archer and Avey plots. Known affectionately as Grandma Gillis by many, she remains in an unmarked grave.

Notable Resident: Hortense Ward

Suffragist attorney Hortense Sparks Ward (1872–1944) was the first woman registered to vote in Harris County. In 1906, she began to practice law with her husband after becoming the first woman to pass the Texas state bar exam. Fearing that all-male juries might react poorly to a female lawyer, Ward chose to work behind the scenes. She became a prominent campaigner for women's suffrage and women's rights, writing multiple pamphlets and newspaper articles on the subject while also achieving many firsts in her own right. She would become, in 1915, the first woman below the Mason-Dixon line to be admitted to practice before the United States Supreme Court. After registering to vote on June 27, the first woman to do so in Harris County, she helped persuade another 386,000 women in the state to register in just seventeen days.

Notable Resident: Julia Ideson

Famed Houston librarian Julia Bedford Ideson (1880–1945) served the Houston community in her role for forty years. Ideson was born in Nebraska; her father owned a bookstore in Hastings until moving the family to Houston when she was twelve. Seeking to become a teacher, she attended the University of Texas at Austin but changed to a new course of study in her second year: library science. On graduation, she was appointed head librarian of the new Houston Lyceum and Carnegie Library in 1903, a position she would hold for over four decades.

The vision of, and choices made by, Julia Ideson resonate with Houstonians young and old to this day. Following graduation from UT–Austin, she was appointed head librarian of Houston's new Lyceum and Carnegie Library. She would hold this position for over four decades and transformed the way Houston's library system served the community. *Courtesy of Special Collections, University of Houston Libraries.*

Ideson became involved in numerous political and social issues. She was a proponent of professional opportunities for women and led a primarily female staff; traveled to France to help establish a library for African American soldiers in 1919; created the Houston Open Forum, a speaker series discussing controversial topics; and served on a committee to reevaluate the city charter for Houston to better interact with the community in educational and entertaining ways.

At the time of her death in 1945, Ideson had increased the Houston Public Library's collection from just over 13,000 volumes to nearly 266,000, with its annual circulation rising tenfold from 60,000 to 600,000. Her efforts to improve the library system's physical facilities resulted in the addition of five branches, a new Central Library and the first municipal bookmobile in the state. Her original Central Library, which served as the sole main library building from 1926 to 1976, now houses the Houston Metropolitan Research Center and contains the library's archives, manuscripts and the Texas and Local History Center. The downtown Houston Spanish Renaissance–style building is named in her honor.

NOTABLE RESIDENT: SHINPEI MYKAWA

Shinpei Mykawa (1874–1906) came to the United States in 1903 after graduating from college. He arrived as a naval officer representing the Japanese navy at the St. Louis World's Fair, passing through Houston on his return trip to Japan. He found that the land around Houston would be perfect for rice cultivation. Returning in 1906 with four men, he settled in an unincorporated part of Harris County called Erin Station and established a rice farm. His work introduced rice agriculture to not only the Houston area but also large parts of Southeast Texas. He died in 1906 after falling underneath one of his pieces of agricultural equipment. The Santa Fe Railroad Co. renamed Erin Station to Mykawa in his honor; today, it is emblazoned with his name. Following the Japanese attack on Pearl Harbor, Hollywood Cemetery placed Mykawa's gravestone in hiding for safekeeping after receiving threats against his grave.

On a trip to St. Louis representing the Japanese navy, Shinpei Mykawa found that the land around Houston was perfect for rice cultivation. His introduction of the process changed the agricultural look of large parts of southeast Texas. *Author's collection.*

NOTABLE RESIDENT: MOLLIE ARLINE KIRKLAND BAILEY

Confederate spy and the so-called Circus Queen of the Southwest, Mollie Arline Kirkland Bailey's (1841–1918) grave is located not by a headstone but a historical marker. Known as Aunt Mollie, Bailey was born on an Alabama plantation, expressing a talent for performing and putting on plays as a child. A bit of a tomboy, Bailey was enrolled in a Tuscaloosa ladies' academy to help "civilize" her tendencies.

As a teen, Mollie met cornet player James "Gus" Bailey, who came from a circus family. The two eloped, stealing a wagon and several horses from her family to get away; Mollie was disinherited as a result. The couple joined a handful of Gus's family members, performing in Alabama, Arkansas and Mississippi as the Bailey Family Troupe until the Civil War broke out.

Gus enlisted in the Confederate army, while Mollie became a nurse and, reportedly, a spy for John Bell Hood and Jubal Early, leaving their daughter, Dixie, with friends in Virginia to do so. In 1864, Gus and Mollie, along with her brother-in-law Alfred, joined back up to perform, this time as part of Hood's Minstrels. They enjoyed growing fame, especially through a march Gus wrote during his time in the Army, "The Old Grey Mare." The song became so popular that it served as the official marching song of the Texas Brigade and the theme song for the 1928 Democratic convention.

Here lies Mollie Bailey, founder and operator of circus companies. Her Mollie A. Bailey Show grew to include thirty-one wagons and over two hundred animals and promised the absence of any con games on the midway. The historic marker is the best estimation of her burial, which would be behind it in the unmarked stretch of land. *Author's collection.*

Following the war, Mollie and Gus began touring as the Bailey Concert Company, performing first on showboats until 1879 and then officially as a circus. When Gus fell ill, Mollie overtook operations, calling it the Mollie A. Bailey Show and offering free admission to indigent children and all veterans from both sides. Beginning as a one-ring circus, at its peak, it grew to include thirty-one wagons and over two hundred animals and prided itself on the absence of the con games that were predominant at the time. Following the death of her daughter, Mollie retired from the circus in 1917 but continued to manage the operation by telegraphy. Following her 1918 death at Houston's St. Joseph's Infirmary, the circus, lacking her guidance, closed within two years. She is buried in the Fountain Hill section.

Chapter 16

HOLY CROSS CEMETERY

3502 North Main Street
Houston

Located adjacent to Hollywood Cemetery, Holy Cross sits just north of Main Street. It is in full sight—and sound—of Interstate 45 on the north side of downtown. Outside of a good handful of trees, the landscaping and foliage is limited, leaving much of the design to the cemetery monuments themselves.

HISTORY

Holy Cross Cemetery is Houston's second-oldest Catholic cemetery. While it was formally established sometime prior to 1904, its grave markers date as far back as 1878. It was established when the St. Vincent's Cemetery on Navigation in East Houston started to fill and had to restrict burials. A yellow fever epidemic filled space in Glenwood and St. Vincent's and, later Holy Cross, so much that new space was needed.

Created by Church of the Annunciation pastor Father Thomas Hennessey, Holy Cross covers twelve acres and is owned by the Catholic Archdiocese of Houston-Galveston, which maintain it as well as five other graveyards in the area. It has become the burial ground of bishops, clergy and a diverse group of church faithful and is ethnically and racially diverse. Headstones reflecting Houstonians with heritage that is German, Irish, African American, Italian, Czech, Polish, Hispanic and Lebanese can easily be tracked down here.

This stained-glass window is one of three like it, all placed along the wall near the entry to Holy Cross Cemetery. This is Houston's second oldest Catholic cemetery, with grave markers dating to 1878, nearly thirty years before the cemetery's formal establishment. *Author's collection.*

LOCAL CELEBRITY

Jerry Denny, Old Judge Cigarettes Card, 1887. *Courtesy Metropolitan Museum of Art, the Jefferson R. Burdick Collection, Gift of Jefferson R. Burdick.*

Born Jeremiah Dennis Eldridge, JERRY DENNY (1859–1927) was a major league third baseman for thirteen years, playing for the Philadelphia Phillies and the New York Giants along with a handful of bygone teams such as the Providence Grays, the St. Louis Maroons, the Indianapolis Hoosiers, the Cleveland Spiders and the Louisville Cardinals. He was one of the few ambidextrous players at the time, and when fielding gloves gradually gained acceptance between the mid-1880s and mid-1890s, Denny refused to compromise; he continued to play without one until he was the final holdout, finishing out his career having never taken the field sporting a glove. After leaving the majors in 1894, he continued playing minor league ball until 1902.

NOTABLE RESIDENT: MAURICE SULLIVAN

Maurice Sullivan (1884–1961) trained as a civil engineer at Detroit College and the University of Michigan before finding work with Fort Worth architects Waller, Shaw and Field and for the Waco architects Scott and Pearson. He moved to Houston in 1912 and became the city's official architect until 1919, educating himself informally in architectural design before beginning his own independent architecture practice. His first important work, the Villa de Matel for the Sisters of Charity of the Incarnate Word in Houston, led to

The magnitude of the Villa de St. Matel came from the architectural work of Maurice Sullivan. For much of his career, he specialized in designing buildings for Catholic religious orders of the Diocese of Galveston. *Courtesy of Special Collections, University of Houston Libraries.*

a specialization in the design of religious, educational and medical buildings for Catholic religious orders and institutions of the Diocese of Galveston. His work was eclectic, and in it you can find an array of genres, such as Lombard Romanesque, Mediterranean and neo-Gothic.

Sullivan worked alone as well as with others on many projects. He shared an office with architect Birdsall P. Briscoe from 1919 to 1955; together, they designed such structures as the 1936 Stephen F. Austin High School and the 1940 Ripley House. Additionally, Sullivan worked with Alfred Bossom on the 1926 Petroleum Building and with Hobart Upjohn on the 1949 Presbyterian church. Among the best-known buildings of Sullivan's own design are the 1927 Sacred Heart Dominican Convent, the 1931 Houston Negro Hospital School of Nursing, the 1940 St. Thomas High School and the 1954 St. Mary's Seminary.

NOTABLE RESIDENT: BARTHOLOMEW D'ASTI

Bartholomew (Rev. Augustine) D'Asti (1827–1866) was Houston's Franciscan missionary to the poor. He spent much of his young life doing missionary work in Italy and studying for doctorates in theology and philosophy at the University of Turin. When he decided to move to the United States in 1856, he and four Franciscan companions traveled there, established a house for their order in New York and built a seminary, a convent for women and what is now St. Bonaventure University.

In 1860, Bishop Jean M. Odin of Galveston wrote back to New York, asking if anyone would be willing to move to his diocese. He was looking for help reopening the now-empty missions following the Texas Revolution. D'Asti and two other Franciscan priests took up the offer, arriving in Houston that May. D'Asti was assigned a pastorate at St. Vincent's Church, becoming the first Franciscan to work in Texas since the Spanish friars were forced to leave in 1832. He became beloved in the city as he began walking the streets, begging for funds from merchants and the wealthy and giving the money to John Kennedy, owner of a trading post downtown, who would then distribute it to the needy, allowing D'Asti to remain anonymous.

D'Asti was already in poor health when he was appointed pastor of St. Vincent's, potentially from poisoning by water from a lead pipe. He eventually succumbed at the age of thirty-nine shortly after the close of the Civil War. Most businesses in Houston closed for his funeral. The intent was to send his remains back to Allegheny, New York, for burial in the Franciscan cemetery there, but when many Houston residents vociferously objected, he was instead buried on the grounds at St. Vincent's Church. In 1878, when St. Vincent's Cemetery moved to Navigation Boulevard, his body was moved there. He was moved again in 1915 to Holy Cross, where his grave remained unmarked until a headstone was donated in 1953. Now, he is buried with eighteen other priests in a Holy Cross mausoleum.

Chapter 17

HOUSTON NATIONAL CEMETERY

10410 Veterans Memorial Drive Houston

Located in the north part of the city, the Houston National Cemetery can be found just south of the Sam Houston Tollway/Beltway 8 and west of Interstate 45. It is dotted with numerous lakes and trees, and its orderliness and uniformity are a sight to be seen.

History

Established on December 7, 1965, the anniversary of the bombing of Pearl Harbor, as a Veterans Administration Cemetery, it became the Houston National Cemetery in 1973, following the passage of the National Cemetery Act. It was the only government cemetery constructed in the United States during the 1960s. Still active, Houston National Cemetery contains roughly 111,000 grave sites.

At the time of its construction, the cemetery was the largest of its kind. It was designed entirely by Veterans Administration (VA) staff and was the only VA cemetery not located on the grounds of a VA hospital. Prior to this location, the last VA cemetery had been established at the Eagle Point VA Medical Center in Oregon in 1952. The Houston facility has been compared regularly to the one in Arlington, Virginia. At 429 acres, Houston National Cemetery was only slightly smaller than Arlington's 450-plus acres. At the time, the closest in size were a cemetery in Los Angeles, at 114 acres, and the cemetery at Fort Leavenworth in Kansas, at 113 acres.

Row upon row of white headstones dot the landscape of the Houston National Cemetery. It was the only government cemetery constructed in the 1960s and the largest one of its kind. *Author's collection.*

The National Cemetery's Hemicycle serves as a hub at the entrance to the cemetery. At various spots outside the hemicycle's structure are four markers denoting the site of the cemetery's four Medal of Honor recipients. *Author's collection.*

The Hemicycle

The Hemicycle is the largest memorial and most visible structure in Houston National Cemetery and is one of only three of its kind located in national cemeteries. The others are located at Arlington and at the Manila American Cemetery and Memorial in the Philippines. This semicircular monument surrounds a chapel and seventy-five-foot-high bell tower and a large courtyard. Located in the center of the hemicycle are the chapel, the carillon and the speakers' stand. Rice University professor of art David Parsons sculpted a twenty-by-six-foot bas relief made of crushed quartz. It depicts three forms, a fallen soldier supported by two comrades. The bell tower features a 305-bell Schulmerich Americana carillon and was dedicated on May 30, 1970.

Local Celebrities

Located here are four Medal of Honor recipients. Three of them were honored for their service during the Second World War: army captain (then first lieutenant) James Fields (1920–1970) for his actions near Rechicourt,

Macario Garcia received his Medal of Honor in a ceremony at the White House. Private Garcia was wounded in action at Normandy, rejoined his unit and on November 27, 1944, earned his medal near Grosshau, Germany. He single-handedly assaulted two German machine-gun emplacements blocking his company's advance. While wounded, he managed to kill six enemy soldiers, capture four and destroy the nests with grenades. *Courtesy of National Archives.*

France; army sergeant major (then private) Macario Garcia (1920–1972) for his actions near Grosshau, Germany; and army air corps first lieutenant Raymond Knight (1922–1945) for his actions spanning two days over the northern Po Valley, Italy area. Army first sergeant David McNerney (1931–2010) received his Medal of Honor for his actions near Polei Doc during the Vietnam War.

Lisa Gaye (1935–2016) made her first film appearance at age seven. By the age of seventeen, she had signed a seven-year contract with Universal Studios, appearing in thirteen films. Gaye also appeared on stage and in television. Her best-known roles were in the film *Drums Across the River* (1954) and on TV in *The George Burns and Gracie Allen Show* and *Perry Mason*, in a career that culminated with an appearance on *The Mod Squad* in 1970. Her husband passed in 1977, and in 1988, she moved permanently to Texas, where two of her sisters lived.

Famed R&B pianist Amos Milburn (1927–1980) earned thirteen battle stars in the Philippines during the Second World War while in the navy before returning to Houston, where he organized a sixteen-piece band. In 1946, Milburn signed with Aladdin Records out of Los Angeles, spending eight years with the company and releasing seventy-five recordings, including "Hold Me Baby" and "Chicken Shack Boogie," which reached the Billboard Top Ten in 1949. He was a popular touring artist, frequently playing the Rudy Toombs–penned "One Scotch, One Bourbon, One Beer," a cover favorite of numerous blues artists. He returned to Houston in 1956, where he formed his band, fell out of favor on the radio and was eventually dropped from the label. His final recording was for a 1972 album by Johnny Otis, shortly after being impaired by a stroke. A second stroke resulted in the amputation of a leg and, at the age of fifty-two, a third stroke took his life.

Hazel Juanita Shofner Wilson (1918–1966) lived for most of her life in Houston. She joined the war effort in September 1943, the first woman from Houston to enlist in the U.S. Navy Reserve Corps, or WAVES (Women Accepted for Volunteer Emergency Service). She served from 1943 to 1948 and obtained the rank of chief yeoman, finishing her career at the Naval Training Center in Great Lakes, Illinois, before returning to Houston. She was the first woman to be buried at the Houston National Cemetery.

Baseball Hall of Famer Willard Brown (1915–1996) is another famed Negro League baseball player laid to rest at Houston National. Nicknamed "Home Run" Brown, he played outfield with the Kansas City Monarchs before making it to the majors as a member of the St. Louis Browns. While with Kansas City, he led the Negro American League in hits for eight seasons, tying Tigers slugger Ty Cobb for the most in baseball history, and he would also tie Josh Gibson for leading in runs batted in seven times, second best in

Wilbur "Home Run" Brown, seen here with Ted Strong, played for the powerhouse Kansas City Monarchs. Eventually he made his way to the majors with the St. Louis Browns, becoming the first African American player to hit a home run in the American League. *Courtesy of Library of Congress.*

baseball history. He holds the distinction of being the first African American player to hit a home run in the American League. He played in the Mexican and Puerto Rican Leagues and in Canada, Venezuela, the Dominican League and the Texas and Western Leagues before retiring in 1958 following a barnstorming series with the Monarchs. He has been named to the MLB, Puerto Rico and Caribbean Halls of Fame.

Notable Resident: Dan Bankhead

Major League Baseball's first African American pitcher was Dan Bankhead (1920–1976). He was playing in the Negro Leagues when World War II broke out and signed up with the Marine Corps Reserves from 1942 to 1946, playing for the Montford Point baseball team at Camp Lejeune, North Carolina, and touring the nation to help raise morale and support for the war effort. Surrounding the war, he played for the Birmingham Black

Barons and the Memphis Red Sox from 1940 to 1947, matching up against such familiar foes as his brothers Sam, Fred, Joe and Garnett, all of whom played in the league as well.

When Bankhead joined the Brooklyn Dodgers in 1947, he followed Jackie Robinson, Larry Doby, Hank Thompson and Willard Brown but was the first Black pitcher to make the majors. He pitched with the team in 1947 and again in 1950–51. Although he struggled somewhat with his command, he amassed a record of 20–9, and some of his struggles, which were not present in the Negro or minor leagues, were attributed to nervousness about any reaction that might arise from a Black pitcher beaning a White hitter in the bigs. He would later spend time with various teams in the Mexican League before retiring in 1966.

Notable Resident: George McElroy

Pioneering African American journalist George Albert McElroy (1922–2006) earned a list of firsts during his life. His father, Hugh McElroy, was a highly decorated war veteran, and George followed in his father's footsteps, receiving an appointment as an information specialist back in Houston at Ellington Air Force Base after World War II.

Following his discharge, George chose to stay in segregated Texas, where he was denied admission to the University of Texas and instead forced to attend Texas State University for Negroes (today's Texas Southern University), where he would receive his journalism degree and would later become the first African American to receive a master's in journalism at the University of Missouri. In 1937, McElroy had already started his journalism career, becoming a youth columnist for the oldest African American newspaper in the state, the *Informer*. He continued an on-again, off-again tenure with the paper for fifty-eight years, eventually serving as editor emeritus until his death in 2006. He also worked for the *Houston Post* as a sportswriter in 1954, becoming a weekly columnist in 1956, the first Black reporter and columnist at what was the largest morning paper in the state.

One of McElroy's focuses remained civil rights. In 1960, McElroy was contacted by thirteen students planning a sit-in at a local Weingarten store. McElroy informed the leader, Eldreway Stearns, that he would send a photographer from the *Informer* and that they should call the police themselves. When over one people eventually participated, his tip turned out to be fortuitous as it resulted in a protest that ended peacefully and with the Houston television and printed press dubbing it the "first sit-in west of the Mississippi."

Well known, McElroy would serve as the Texas correspondent for *Jet Magazine* and president of the Press Club of Houston, interviewing the likes of Martin Luther King Jr., Fidel Castro and six American presidents, among a slew of others. Additionally, he taught at Phyllis Wheatley and Jack Yates High Schools, the University of Houston and Texas Southern University. He died shortly after being presented with the Lifetime Achievement Award from the Houston Association of Black Journalists.

Notable Resident: Kermit Beahan

Career air force officer Kermit Beahan (1918–1989) made quite the name for himself in World War II. Beahan's bombardier skills were said to be so precise he could "hit a pickle barrel with a bomb from 30,000 feet." He had played football at Rice University before joining the United States Army Air Forces in 1939, where he washed out of pilot training and swapped over to becoming a bombardier instead. He flew multiple missions over Europe and North Africa and in the Pacific. During these tours, he was shot down and crash landed four times, twice in Europe and twice in North Africa.

By the summer of 1944, Beahan had returned to the States, locating in Midland, Texas, to become a bombing instructor. There he was recruited by Colonel Paul Tibbets to become a part of his 509th Composite Group, formed to deliver the atomic bomb to Japan. He participated in the first atomic mission on August 6, dropping "Little Boy" over Hiroshima, Japan. Three days later, he served as the bombardier on the crew flying the Boeing B-29 Superfortress Bockscar to Nagasaki with "Fat Man" as their payload. The mission faced failure as they neared the Japanese target. Admiral Frederick L. Ashworth, participating as the mission's weaponeer, credited Beahan with saving the mission. Kermit found an opening in the clouds, allowing them to complete the required visual bombing of the city. The blast would kill between thirty-five and forty thousand on impact.

After the war, Beahan returned to the States. He remained in the United States Air Force until his retirement as a lieutenant in 1964. In his post-military career, he worked as a technical writer for the engineering and construction firm Brown & Root.

The flight crew of the Bocks Car, pictured here, included Kermit Beahan. Beahan participated in the first atomic mission on August 6, dropping "Little Boy" over Hiroshima and its follow-up, "Fat Man," over Nagasaki. *Courtesy of Library of Congress.*

Notable Resident: Albert Thomas

After enlisting and serving as a lieutenant in the U.S. Army during World War I, Albert Thomas (1898–1966) returned to his home state of Texas following the war. He graduated from Rice University and law school, gained admittance to the bar in 1927, practiced in Nacogdoches and became a county attorney before moving to Houston in 1930 to become the assistant U.S. attorney for the Southern District of Texas.

When longtime congressman Joe Eagle decided not to seek reelection in 1936 so he could run for the U.S. Senate, Thomas sought and won the Democratic nomination from Houston mayor Oscar Holcombe in an upset.

Thomas would become a protege of fellow Texan Lyndon Baines Johnson and serve on the subcommittees on independent office appropriations and defense appropriations and on the joint committee on Texas House delegation. His efforts helped steer projects to Texas including the construction of the Corpus Christi Naval Air Station and NASA's Manned Spacecraft Center, located on Houston land donated by Brown & Root, the company founded by George R. Brown, Thomas's college roommate.

Accompanying his mentor and then vice president, Thomas was in John F. Kennedy's presidential party when it arrived in Houston and left for Dallas and acted as a witness to the swearing in of LBJ as president on Air Force One. When Thomas died a few years later, in 1966, his wife, Lera Thomas, completed his term, the first woman to represent Texas in the United States House of Representatives. Thomas's office is depicted in an exhibit outside the entrance to Houston's Bayou Place, formerly known as the Albert Thomas Convention & Exhibit Center.

Chapter 18

IMPERIAL FARM CEMETERY

Highway 90 and Hwy 6
Sugar Land

You might miss it if you aren't looking for this cemetery. Located in a field south of Highway 90 in Sugar Land, the cemetery is set back from Easton Avenue and fenced off, with the only interpretation coming from a historical marker located nearby. Originally it was located outside Sugar Land's corporate limits; however, the prison cemetery and surrounding property were dedicated to the city in 2006. Inside the fenced area are several crumbling headstones, inscribed with names and prisoner numbers.

History

The history of the cemeteries on this and surrounding land is a complicated one. In the years following the Civil War and the emancipation of the enslaved, Southern plantation owners and businessmen found themselves scrambling to find a replacement for their labor force. When they realized that the protection of African Americans through emancipation did not extend to those who had been convicted of crimes and subsequently sentenced to prison, a system was developed that included prison labor. Prisoners would be leased to businessmen from the state, giving them access to this low-cost, unregulated labor market.

Demand quickly exceeded the number of people breaking the law. To meet that demand, African Americans found themselves being arrested for the most minor of crimes such as vagrancy or simply walking along railroad tracks. The conditions for these individuals were no better than the ones experienced by slaves. With no oversight or regulation, dangerous situations resulted, at times, in death. The profitability of the program for both the government and the businesses was just too high, and it took negative publicity to finally abolish the convict leasing system in the early twentieth century. Convict labor still exists, although using highly modified models, in places like Mississippi.

This land was a Stephen Austin land grant in 1828. Samuel Williams dubbed it Oakland Plantation after the variety of oak trees in the area and grew corn, cotton and sugarcane here until 1853. Benjamin Terry and William Kyle purchased the plantation and continued the practice before selling it to E.H. Cunningham, who began the development of a sugar refinery. Then, in 1908, Isaac Kempner and William Eldridge bought the property and created the Imperial Sugar Company, growing a company town up around the land. Both involuntary servitude and convict leasing were utilized to work the former plantation and surrounding town development. Convicts were leased from the nearby Imperial State Prison Farm, which the state opened in 1909 on land previously belonging to the sugar company.

In 1930, the prison farm was renamed Central State Prison Farm and continued to expand thereafter. By the 1950s, over one thousand inmates resided there, and the land was transferred and sold, resulting in the further development of Sugar Land's neighborhoods. By 2011, the 5,200-acre prison farm had shrunk to roughly 330 acres, with an announcement of closure that August. The remaining inmates were spread throughout Texas, with more than a few landing in the nearby Jester State prison farm units.

The prisons were essentially microcosmic communities, bringing about the need for cemeteries. The primary marked cemetery contains the burial site of convicts, many of them White. The burial site of the Sugar Land 95, the Bullhead Camp Cemetery, was for African Americans. In the former, there are at least thirty-three known grave sites, the earliest dating from 1912. Three graves are post-dated in the 1930s. The cemeteries would contain the remains of prisoners and guards who died between 1912 and 1942 at the Texas Department of Corrections Central Prison Unit.

The Bullhead Camp burials were not discovered until 2018, although they had long been suspected to exist. Ninety-five bodies were discovered during the early stages of construction for a Fort Bend Independent School District building in the area near the Old Imperial Farm Cemetery. Forensics has since concluded that these bodies are those of ninety-four African American men and one African American woman. Their ages are all consistent with victims of Sugar Land's convict leasing system, dating from 1878 to 1910. Adding support to the identification of the remains as such was the discovery of chains and other prison-related artifacts.

Known Burials

Fred Carson (1889–1917): Born in Oklahoma, convict no. 29760—alias Frank Walker, convict no. 26315—was a White laborer who had resided in Terrell, Texas. He spent time in numerous facilities, including Imperial more than once, prior to his last stint there, which started in September 1913. Carson had escaped multiple times, generally during transit, but was eventually caught after each attempt. He died of obstruction of the bowels.

Taylor L. Odom (1897–1927): Prisoner 54714. Odom drowned while attempting to escape.

The Imperial Prison Farm cemetery was used for the Central State Prison Farm, located just north of this site. This area, once a plantation, was eventually bought out and incorporated by the Imperial Sugar Company. Conditions on these lend-lease operations were so bad that injuries and death was not uncommon. *Author's collection.*

RICHARD COLEMAN (1924–1943): Convict no. 99479 was a former farmer and blacksmith and was arrested for theft in 1942. He had been incarcerated for only nineteen days at Imperial Farm when he died. He received a gunshot wound in the left side of his chest from the sergeant of the guards. In that short amount of time, Coleman purposely severed his right Achilles tendon and received eight days in solitary for using "profane" language and for instigating a riot.

JOE DORSEY (1884–1917): Convict no. 30736 and ex-convict no. 26758. Joe was convicted of the murder of Tilden Goode, along with Ed Beard and Mrs. Tilden Goode, and sentenced to hang in February 1910. The governor would later commute that to life imprisonment. Dorsey spent time at Huntsville, Ramsey, Clemens Farm and Blue Ridge and died of pneumonia.

NOTABLE RESIDENT: THE SUGARLAND 95

The Sugar Land 95 were laborers in the Bullhead Convict Labor Camp. A cemetery for these individuals was established by the prison. However, over the years, it was abandoned and lay hidden for decades, lost to time and memory. The Bullhead Camp laborers once played a fundamental role in building up Fort Bend County and the city of Sugar Land. Following the discovery of the cemetery and the bioarchaeological and historical research that followed, the names of seventy-two of the ninety-four men who died at Bullhead Camp between 1879 and 1909 were identified, although no names have yet been attached to the individual remains.

The Sugar Land 95 were ninety-four men and one woman whose burial sites were disturbed by the Fort Bend Independent School District during a construction project. A lengthy battle over the remains and site resulted in a permanent burial site complete with markers, like this one, and a protective fence. *Author's collection.*

The story of these men—their conviction, imprisonment, treatment, death and discovery—has since been added into the district's social studies curriculum. Following a ceremony held in November 2019, the remains of the Sugar Land 95 were reburied at the same site where they were found. Prior to reburial, each site and vessel was marked so that individuals could be reunified with family should any descendants be identified. Additionally, work has been done with the local historical organizations to help interpret the stories of these individuals and the convict leasing program through exhibits placed in the county. A permanent marker has been added to the site. The Houston Museum of Natural Science—which is housed inside what was once the main unit, known as Two Camp, where the prison's Black inmates were held—now includes an exhibit documenting the prisoners' contributions, and the city of Sugar Land is protecting and maintaining the prison cemetery property.

Chapter 19

MORTON CEMETERY

401 North Second Street
Richmond

Located north of downtown Richmond, off second street, Morton Cemetery is peppered with trees, especially some very large oak trees. While it still appears to hold some of its rural, small-town charm, don't let that fool you. Morton is good sized and very well maintained.

History

Located on over fifteen acres, Richmond's Morton Cemetery is one of the most historic cemeteries in the state. It was established on the family land of William Morton when Texas was still part of Mexico. In November 1821, five men of the first installment of Morton's new colony built a fort in the bend of the Brazos River, near the present-day town of Richmond. The fort was built for shelter, to keep supplies and for defense in case of any attack. Morton was the first settler to the area, with his league located on the east side of the river and his labor on the west side near the fort (the location of the cemetery), both granted to him by the Mexican government in 1824.

Following a major flood in 1833, Morton disappeared, his body never to be recovered. His widow sold the land, in part and parcel, to a variety of people over the years. In 1854, a portion was sold to Michael DeChaumes and his wife, who established a cemetery around the grave site of Robert Gillespie, a traveler from Scotland who passed away from an illness and was buried by William Morton on his land. A portion of the DeChaumes Cemetery later became the Richmond Masonic Cemetery. The masons continued to expand the cemetery, a practice continued by Mamie George with additional land deeded in 1963. Today, it is the final resting place for over 3,200 individuals and continues to be active.

MEMORABLE HEADSTONES

The grave of Morton's visitor Robert Gillespie (1780–1825) is unique. William Morton ensured Gillespie's grave included a monument engraved with Masonic society symbols. He wanted to indicate in perpetuity the man's membership in the group. Gillespie was a traveler from Scotland who perished due to an illness in 1825. Morton had been providing shelter to Gillespie when he died and buried him in a tomb on the property. The story goes that in April 1836, Santa Anna and his army camped near this site prior to crossing the Brazos River on their way to an eventual battle at San Jacinto. Soldiers used ropes to pull the monument off the plumb of its foundation, an offense given the Masonic nature of the tomb. It remained like this for one hundred years, until 1836, when it was rebuilt by members of the Morton Mason Lodge. Inside the tomb was placed a time capsule crafted of copper. It is thought to be the oldest Masonic monument in the state.

The unique grave of Robert Gillespie, a wanderer who died while on the land of William Morton. The grave includes this monument engraved with Masonic society symbols. Gillespie had been ill, and Morton provided the Scottish traveler shelter. When Gillespie died, Morton buried him on the property. *Author's collection.*

LOCAL CELEBRITIES

MARY E. "MAMIE" DAVIS GEORGE (1877–1971) and ALBERT PEYTON GEORGE (1873–1955) were married in 1896, living their lives on a ranch about nine miles south of town. Albert was a local businessman who was active in ranching and banking and served as a county commissioner. He had a primary interest in raising livestock that eventually culminated in his own breed of cattle (Brahorn). He also owned the World Champion Show Herd of Shorthorn Cattle and was one of the founders of the Houston Fat Stock Show, which lives on as the Houston Livestock and Rodeo Show.

Mamie outlived her husband by over a dozen years and was known to Fort Bend County as Miss Mamie. Her lineage traced back to Henry Jones, one of the First Three Hundred Austin colonists. She supported individuals and organizations through her charitable efforts, many of which were never publicized. The A.P. George Foundation still operates and is highly influential in Houston's philanthropic community, supporting a wide range of efforts. These have included the Polly Ryon Memorial Hospital, numerous parks and this very cemetery.

Hilmar Moore (1920–2012), at the time of his death, was the longest-serving mayor in the history of the United States. Moore was appointed to fill an unexpired term as the mayor of Richmond on September 22, 1949, winning thirty-two consecutive elections thereafter and serving for a total of sixty-three years in the role.

At the time of his death, Hilmar Moore was the longest-serving mayor in the history of the United States. What started out as an appointment to an unfilled seat turned into a sixty-three-year-long legacy in one of the most diverse areas of the United States. *Author's collection.*

Born in North Carolina, former slave Walter Moses Burton (1840–1913) became an early influential African American figure in Texas history. Burton was brought to Texas about 1860 and, after the Civil War, purchased land from his former owner, Thomas B. Burton, from whom he had learned to read and write. A successful and well-known local farmer, Burton campaigned for and was elected sheriff of Fort Bend County. Following this, he was elected to the Texas senate in 1873, serving four terms and representing Fort Bend, Austin, Waller and Wharton Counties. After retiring his seat in the senate in 1882, Burton returned to farming in Fort Bend, remaining active in local politics until his death in 1913.

Soldier, blacksmith and Fort Bend County sheriff Thomas Jefferson Smith (1808–1890) was orphaned as a small child in Virginia and reared in Georgia by relatives. As a member of the Georgia

Battalion, he entered Texas in 1835, fighting at the siege of Bexar and then the Battle of Refugio before being captured near Victoria. While he was twice wounded, he managed to escape the Goliad Massacre, spared to repair guns for the Mexican army. He managed to escape in April and was honorably discharged a few months later. After the revolution, he settled in Richmond, operated a blacksmith shop and ran a hotel and a livery stable. He would serve the county as its sheriff from 1853 to 1857.

NOTABLE RESIDENT: MIRABEAU BUONAPARTE LAMAR

Mirabeau Buonaparte Lamar (1798–1859) served as the second president of the Republic of Texas. Born in Georgia, Lamar established an illustrious young career there before moving to Texas. An expert horseman, fencer, speaker and poet, he established Muscogee County's *Columbus Enquirer* newspaper and was elected state senator in 1829. Following the deaths of his first wife and a son, he began to travel, eventually leaving Georgia for Texas in 1835.

This monument marks the grave of the second president of the Republic of Texas. Mirabeau Lamar came to Texas a Renaissance man, having already established an illustrious career and skilled as a horseman, fencer, speaker and poet. He would also serve as commander in chief of the Texas army and secretary of war. *Author's collection.*

Initially, Lamar's goal in traveling to Texas was only to collect historical data for his journal. However, while on a trip to Georgia in order to make the move a permanent one, he rushed back when word of the Alamo falling and the Goliad Massacre came through. He joined the army on his return, enlisting as a private. Before the Battle of San Jacinto, he managed to save Thomas J. Rusk and Walter Paye Lane, receiving a verbal commission as a colonel and being assigned to command the cavalry for his efforts.

Following the battle, Lamar was appointed secretary of war and, later, commander in chief of the Texas army. In September 1836, he was elected the republic's vice president and then followed Sam Houston as its second president, serving until 1841. Some of his efforts included the controversial eradication of the Cherokees from

Texas, but he also has been called the father of Texas public education, started the Homestead Law of Texas and is responsible for relocating the state capital to Austin.

After the presidency and following the deaths of his mother and his daughter, Lamar started traveling again and eventually remarried in 1851. He fought in the battle of Monterrey during the Mexican War. In 1857, Lamar was appointed the United States minister to Nicaragua and Costa Rica. In 1859, he returned to his plantation in Richmond, where he died later that year.

NOTABLE RESIDENT: JANE LONG

Known as the Mother of Texas, Jane Herbert Wilkinson Long (1798–1880) followed her husband, Dr. James Long, to help free Texas in 1820. The Longs settled at Bolivar Point in 1820, where they established an outpost in the hopes of helping free Texas from Spanish rule. When Dr. Long left on an excursion in 1821, Jane stayed behind and vowed to remain at the fort until his return. Instead of returning, he was captured and killed in Mexico City.

Jane Long, the "Mother of Texas," settled with her husband, Dr. James Long, at Bolivar Point in 1820. She continued at the fort despite his capture and killing in Mexico in 1821, staying behind to maintain the semblance of safety and protection at the fort. She remained a widow until her death in 1880. *Courtesy of Special Collections, University of Houston Libraries.*

Unaware of her husband's fate, Jane remained at Bolivar Point throughout that winter. As supplies ran out, the few remaining inhabitants began to leave. Jane, her six-year-old daughter and a twelve-year-old servant survived on a dwindling supply of corn meal, salted fish and oysters they managed to scavenge from Galveston Bay. They kept intruders and attackers at bay by attempting to give the illusion that the fort remained protected by soldiers. The following March, a friend of Jane's husband persuaded her to leave Bolivar Point amid reports that Dr. Long had been killed.

Jane left Texas for the United States. However, in 1832, she returned to the area. She opened a successful hotel in Brazoria, a primary port for newly arriving immigrants to Texas. Her hotel became a focal point for activities social and political in Texas. For nearly sixty years, she rejected all suitors, instead dying a widow.

Notable Resident: William Kinchen Davis

William Kinchen Davis (1822–1891) was an early pioneer of Fort Bend County. Born in Alabama, he came to Texas as an eight-year-old boy and, at the age of fourteen, helped build a fort at the mouth of the Brazos. By 1839, he was involved in local military service, assisting in a campaign against Native Americans around the head of the Brazos.

In 1842, Davis, now a captain, joined the Somerville expedition. This command eventually dissolved at the Rio Grande with a portion, including Davis, proceeding into Mexico, fighting at the disastrous Battle of Mier. During the melee, Davis was severely wounded and marched with other prisoners to the village of Salado. There he joined other Texans as they charged the guards, resulting in a fierce hand-to-hand conflict that culminated in short-lived freedom as they were again captured and marched back to Salado. Davis was one of the lucky ones who drew a white bean, and he was forced to Mexico City and set to hard labor (those who drew a black bean were summarily executed). From there, those who drew a white bean were sent to and imprisoned in the Peyote dungeon before getting their release from Santa Anna. He gave each man one dollar to make the 1,500-mile journey back to Texas, a journey at which Captain Davis eventually succeeded.

Davis would marry Jane Pickens the following year, and they had five children before she died in 1860. He married again after the Civil War, during which he commanded a company that saw no action. During his later years, he became a successful businessman and a leader in Fort County.

Notable Resident: James Long

General James Long (1793–1822) led a short but storied military life. Long joined the United States Army at the outset of the War of 1812, seeking to serve as a surgeon and then, following the Battle of New Orleans, set up practice at Port Gibson in Natchez, Mississippi. He then purchased a plantation near Vicksburg in 1817 and became a merchandising operations partner.

In 1819, Long found himself placed in command of a political filibustering expedition to conquer Texas. The Adams-Onis Treaty, signed between the United States and Spain, gave Florida to the United States and defined the boundary between the Kingdom of New Spain and the United States, thus renouncing the U.S. claim to Texas and generating strong opposition, especially in Natchez. On his arrival in Texas, Long was proclaimed governor of the "Republic of Texas," which lasted four short months. The expedition settled opposite Galveston Island at Bolivar Point, but it was short-lived; many of the group returned after finding the living conditions in Texas too demanding. In October 1821, Long and the remaining men were captured and imprisoned in San Antonio and in Monterrey. Prior to an 1822 pleading of his case in Mexico City, he was "accidentally" shot and killed by a guard. His wife, Jane, following his death, returned to Texas with their children in 1832 and opened a successful hotel.

Chapter 20

OLIVEWOOD CEMETERY

1300 Court Street Houston

Forgotten" or "neglected" would be the appropriate words to use for much of Olivewood's most recent history. However, that's changed as more attention has been focused on this fascinating graveyard located west of downtown Houston and between Interstate 10 and Washington Avenue, now surrounded by new construction. It's tucked away in Houston's Fourth Ward off Studemont, and while it can be difficult to track down, there are multiple signs marking the way.

History

Olivewood Cemetery was founded in the late 1870s by Robert Brock, one of Houston's first Black aldermen. In its early years, it was known as Olive Wood, Hollow Wood and Hollywood. The land had been set aside as a graveyard for freed slaves and opened as an official cemetery for Black Methodists in 1877. It served Houston's early African American community for nearly a century as the first cemetery for Houston's freedmen within the city limits. It covers five and a half acres, with two additional acres added in 1917. White Oak Bayou sits on the northern edge, its erosion likely leading to the loss of an unknown number of grave sites. The original 444 family plots comprise well over 5,000 burial spaces; this number continued to grow throughout the 1960s.

After people stopped utilizing the property, the cemetery rarely saw frequent attention and was essentially forgotten. Weeds and vines grew

Originally set aside for freed slaves following emancipation, Olivewood was Houston's first cemetery for freedmen inside the city limits. In 2022, it was designated as one of the National Historic Preservation Trust's Most Endangered Historical Sites. *Author's collection.*

alongside the massive oak and pecan trees, essentially burying the cemetery itself, making reading or even finding headstones difficult. Today, the cemetery is run by the Descendants of Olivewood Inc. Through the organization's efforts, the cemetery has been reclaimed and cleared, eventually earning the designation as a Historic Texas Cemetery. In 2013, a digital database was created for those buried between 1910 and 1940. New energy and attention were thrown at Olivewood when, in early 2022, it was designated by the National Historic Preservation Trust as one of its Most Endangered Historical Sites, and it is listed as one of UNESCO's Sites of Memory as part of the Slave Route Project.

MEMORABLE HEADSTONES

Houston dentist MILTON BAKER (1838–1905) has one of the more elaborate headstones in Olivewood. The centerpiece angel was placed there by his wife on his death with the inscription, "Sacred to the memory of my beloved husband." Flanking the monument are two stone lions as its protectors.

WILL A. HARRIS (1876–1930) was a Houston laborer. Not much about his headstone tells his life story. However, it does offer a glimpse into the earlier

Flanked by two protective lions, the monument in memory of Houston dentist Milton Baker is one of the most elaborate in Olivewood. The cemetery runs the gamut of both design and cultural influence. Baker's headstone stands out from all its neighbors. *Author's collection.*

The backward tiles at the grave of laborer Will Harris may look like a mistake, but they aren't. In fact, Harris's is one of six sites in Olivewood to use upside down and inverted text. Look closely throughout the cemetery and you can find upright metal pipes, seashell designs, left mementoes and gifts and so much more. *Author's collection.*

nineteenth- and twentieth-century cultural burial traditions of African Americans. Harris's is one of six sites in Olivewood to feature the use of upside down and inverted text, his in the form of blue tiles—an old West African tradition, like the upright metal pipes that border some graves and the seashell designs on headstones. You can see numerous examples of West African traditions at the grave sites in Olivewood, many brought from the religious practices and customs of residents' homelands. Some are symbolic, like the shells—they represent crossing over a body of water, like the Styx, to the afterlife. The upside down or sometimes reversed scripts on markers come from the West African belief system. The verb "to die" translates as "upside down" or "inverted," since death is the opposite of life, and the name of the deceased is spelled backward to reflect how they would see it on the "other side." Shards of a mirror that "corrected" the nameplate were found scattered beneath Harris's headstone. The upright metal pipes represent the journey from the physical world to the spirit world and were thought to convey messages to the dead.

The grave marker of Reverend A.F. Jackson, DD (1844–1889), marks his birth and death dates along with the fact that he was murdered in Dallas. Not much is known about his murder other than that it took place in Dallas and was perpetrated by an African American man named Roberts. Jackson had previously lived in Galveston and San Antonio and served the St. Paul A.M.E. church; he was very well known throughout the African American community.

Local Celebrities

Dr. Charles B. Johnson (1852–1922) was known as the Singing Dentist. In 1927, the musician-dentist wrote an homage to his city, "Houston Is a Grand Old Town." The song would later be chosen and performed in 1976 as Houston's own bicentennial song.

Joseph Vance Lewis (circa 1853–1925), a former slave freed through emancipation, would rise to become a lawyer, earning admission to the U.S. Supreme Court. Born in Terrebonne Parish, Louisiana, near Houma, he was raised on the plantation of Colonel Duncan Stewart Cage Sr. along with hundreds of other slaves. After emancipation, he and roughly two hundred other former slaves remained on the plantation, now as employees. A school was started for the African American children on the plantation, and Lewis was educated there, saved his money from working on the plantation and eventually headed off to college at Leland University. After graduation, he gained admission to the Supreme Court of Michigan, attended the Chicago School of Law and was admitted to every court in Illinois. In 1897, Lewis became the only African American lawyer accepted to the bar of the U.S. Supreme Court. He practiced law in Chicago, New Orleans and finally in Houston, where he established what would become a very successful practice.

Joseph Lewis (circa 1860s–1925), a former Louisiana slave, put himself through school after the death of his parents, eventually becoming a prominent Houston lawyer. Lewis successfully defended a Black client accused of murder, a first for an African American lawyer arguing a case before a Harris County jury. In addition to practicing law in Houston, Lewis spoke throughout the country on the matter of civil rights.

Reverend Van H. McKinney (1865–1928) held an influential position in Houston's African American community in a variety of ways. Following the Civil War, as African Americans moved to establish new communities and set out on more self-sufficient lives, they faced numerous difficulties, including finding insurance and securing loans. Established in 1882, the Ancient Order of Pilgrims set to ease those troubles, and McKinney held the visible role of High Chief Protector in addition to others. He also served as a minister of the McKinney Memorial United Methodist Church in LaMarque and a printer, editor and community activist. As owner-operator of the McKinney & Burke Printing Company, he served as the editor of one of Houston's first Black-owned weekly papers, the *Houston Van*. He used his theological background and beliefs as the foundation for the paper's authority.

Notable Resident: James D. Ryan

The leadership James Delbridge Ryan (1872–1940) provided to the African American educational community in Houston was widespread. He had received his undergraduate degree at Prairie View A&M with courses taken at the University of Chicago, University of California and Columbia University before becoming a teacher in 1890 in the Houston public school system.

In 1900, he started teaching math at the Houston Colored High School (later Jack Yates High), becoming its principal two years later. Ryan sought to improve the quality of education for Black students throughout the state and became involved in a variety of state and local committees and organizations focused on this. While his success was based on an accommodating attitude throughout his career, a stance that would cause a decline in his prestige later in life, he was afforded the highest accolades through much of his career.

Additionally, Ryan served on several local community organizations, a fraternity and in the church choir and owned considerable property throughout Houston. He also hosted the first summer school for Black teachers in 1927 and served on the boards of Emancipation Park, the Houston Negro Hospital, Wiley College (where he earned his master's in 1927) and the Houston Interracial Committee.

Notable Resident: Richard Allen

Born into slavery in Richmond, Virginia, Richard Allen (1830–1909) was taken as a child to Texas when his master emigrated there in 1837. As he grew up under slavery, he gained a strong reputation as a skilled carpenter. Following emancipation, he went into business for himself as a contractor, building a mansion for Houston mayor Joseph R. Morris and one of the first bridges across Buffalo Bayou.

In 1867, Allen entered public service as an agent for the federal Freedmen's Bureau. This organization was created to assist emancipated slaves transition off the plantation and out of enslavement. He also joined the Republican Party, starting a lifelong career in politics. He would go on to represent Harris and Montgomery Counties in the Texas legislature, work to improve public education, establish state pensions for Civil War veterans and run for the United States House of Representatives. Though his bid was unsuccessful, when Allen ran for lieutenant governor in 1878, he became the first African American in Texas to run as a candidate for a statewide office. He would continue to be active in the party, attending state and national conventions as a delegate until 1896.

Outside of politics, Allen founded the Bayou City Bank in Houston, won a street-paving contract with the city in 1872, served as a quartermaster in the Texas militia and was appointed as a U.S. customs officer in Houston.

He also was very active in his church and local community organizations, serving as a trustee of the Gregory Institute; helped purchase and establish Emancipation Park; and led several Juneteenth celebrations.

Notable Resident: Reverend Elias Dibble

Born enslaved in Georgia, the Reverend David Elias Dibble (1811–1885) was brought to Texas in 1837. Self-educated, he was a carpenter by trade, became an anointed preacher in 1864 and grew as a respected community and religious leader throughout his life. The following year, Dibble would become the first Black ordained Methodist minister in the United States when he organized and served as the pastor of Houston's first Freedmen's Methodist congregation, which would later choose the name Trinity Methodist Episcopal Church. Dibble worked with the church trustees to unite families in marriage; organize a church school that operated until 1870, when the Gregory Institute opened; and establish Emancipation Park.

Located near the entrance of Olivewood Cemetery is the grave site of Mary White. According to legend, Mary was engaged to be married. Another man, feeling spurned by her, got jealous and murdered Mary in 1888. She is said to haunt the grounds of the cemetery. *Author's collection.*

Eerie Tales: The Ghost of Mary White

Legend has it that there have been reports of mysterious after-dark sightings and strange movements within Olivewood. One of the most well-known stories is that of the ghost of Mary White. Mary, who was buried at Olivewood in 1888, is said to haunt the grounds. Rumor has it that she was engaged to be married but was murdered on her wedding day by another man who was jealous after being spurned. Sightings of Mary include the ghostly visage of this woman hovering above her own headstone.

Chapter 21

PARADISE NORTH CEMETERY

10401 West Montgomery Road
Houston

Paradise North is the newest cemetery in this book. The Paradise Cemetery Group was established in 1979 and operates five cemeteries: Paradise North, Cemetery Beautiful, Paradise South (where former Houston mayor Lee P. Brown is buried), Golden Gate Cemetery and Oak Park Cemetery.

Local Celebrities

Hattie Mae Whiting White (1916–1993) holds the distinction of being the first African American elected to public office in Texas in the twentieth century. During a time when the city's schools were segregated, the former schoolteacher won a place on the Houston Independent School District board in 1958. She opted to run for election after hearing another parent declare the time had not yet come to have a Black school board member. She received an outpouring of support from African American voters and moderate support from White voters, later recalling that it was the first time Black and White Houstonians worked together on a political campaign. However, it brought her into focus as well. A week before the election, someone shot out her car's windshield, and her family bore witness to having a gasoline-soaked cross set afire in their front yard. Despite this, she fought on, leading efforts to desegregate Houston's schools, maintaining that dual school systems were expensive and, in fact,

Hattie Mae Whiting White made waves in segregated Houston. She holds the distinction of being the first African American elected to public office in the twentieth century. Along the way, she suffered verbal abuse and terroristic acts such as having her windshield shot out and a cross set afire in her front lawn. *Courtesy of Special Collections, University of Houston Libraries.*

not equal at all. She was defeated by conservatives in her bid for a third term and afterward redirected her talents to serving several interracial organizations and continuing to fight for equality. She returned to teaching and retired at age seventy. HISD's administration building is named in her honor.

For ten seasons, from 1964 to 1972 and again in 1975, Willie Frazier (1942–2013) played as a tight end for the Houston Oilers, the San Diego Chargers and the Kansas City Chiefs. He played college ball at the University of Arkansas–Pine Bluff and was drafted by the Oilers. He was selected to the Pro-Bowl three times and is considered one of the most productive receivers in the American Football League. Following his career, he worked as a football coach and police officer for the Houston Independent School District. He suffered from a variety of health issues resulting from his football days, including severe back ailments and dementia.

Power forward and center Dwight Jones (1952–2016) spent time on the court for the Atlanta Hawks, Houston Rockets, Chicago Bulls and LA Lakers in a career that spanned ten years in the NBA. He played college ball for the University of Houston from 1971 to 1973 and was a member of the United States team that lost a controversial gold-medal game to the Soviet Union at the 1972 Summer Olympics in Munich.

Musician Joe Sample (1939–2014) was a pianist-composer and fixture in contemporary jazz for over five decades. Along with saxophonist Wilton Felder, drummer Stix Hooper, trombonist Wayne Henderson and several other musicians, the then Texas Southern University student formed the Jazz Crusaders, playing a hard bop style. By the late 1960s, the band had pioneered a more progressive sound of soul and funk. Their last official recording was *Life in the Modern World* in 1987, following numerous gold and platinum albums. As a solo artist, Sample recorded twenty-one albums and recorded and toured with artists such as Marvin Gaye, Anita Baker, Joni Mitchell, Eric Clapton and B.B. King.

The front and back of musician Joe Sample's elaborate headstone. The front is the towering top of a piano with his personal information and a small piece of sheet music for "True to You"; on the back are the liner notes Sample wrote in 2002 for the album *The Pecan Tree*, with a pecan tree carved into the stone. *Author's collection.*

Cleveland "Big Cat" Williams (1933–1999) was the victim of one of the most famous sports photographs in history. Big Cat fought in big-name fights over the years but none bigger than his match against Muhammad Ali in front of his hometown crowd at the Astrodome on November 14, 1966. At the time, Williams was in his fifteenth professional boxing year; at thirty-three years old and the victim of being shot at point-blank range in a scuffle with police two years earlier, he was aged and nearing the end of his career as professional boxer. In his earlier years, he racked up an early 33–1 record, went three brutal rounds with Bob Satterfield and cleaned up the rings with boxers in the southwest. However, he also began suffering from auditory hallucinations, turned violent in domestic disputes and went AWOL so often from the army that he was considered a deserter, fighting under the assumed name of Eugene Mack and spending many of his later military years in the brig or doing hard labor. He would later fight Sonny Liston (twice) and Ernie Terrell before his fracas with the cops, which resulted in damage to his nerves, colon, bowel, kidneys and more. Despite a storied career, he's best remembered by an overhead photo taken from the rafters of the Astrodome, depicting Williams splayed out at the end of his boxing match with Ali.

Hugh George McElroy (1884–1971) lied about his age, enlisting at the age of fifteen in the Tenth United States Cavalry and becoming one of the famed Buffalo Soldiers. McElroy served in Cuba during the Spanish-American War and afterward in the Philippine Insurrection. After his return, the Tenth found itself in the border campaigns against Francisco "Pancho" Villa, joining General John J. Pershing into Mexico in 1916.

Hugh McElroy became one of the famed Buffalo Soldiers at the young age of fifteen. He fought against Pancho Villa along the border with Mexico and distinguished himself on the field of battle during World War I. During the Second World War, Hugh stepped up to serve again, this time as a speaker and poster model for bond drives, likely the first African American to do so. *Courtesy of Special Collections, University of Houston Libraries.*

During World War I, McElroy landed and fought in France, eventually receiving from French war minister Georges Clemenceau the Croix de Guerre for his actions on the battlefield, one of many honors he would obtain for his service. After his service ended in 1927, he followed his brother Thomas to Houston, where he obtained a job as a hospital orderly. During World War II, he found his way back into service, first as head janitor at Ellington Field and then as a speaker and poster model in bond drives, likely the first African American to appear as an advertisement for U.S. war bonds. Following the war, he worked at a few local recruiting stations before finally retiring permanently. In December 1968, he once again was lauded for his service, this time with his oldest son, when they rescued two children from a burning house near his Houston home. When he died in 1971, a detachment from Fort Sam Houston buried him in Paradise North Cemetery with full military honors.

Notable Resident: Don Robey

Born in Houston, Don Robey (1903–1975) had a lifelong passion for music, and it led him to becoming a major force in the entertainment industry in Houston and beyond. He started out doing promotional work for ballroom dances in Houston, spent three years operating the Harlem Grill in Los Angeles during the late 1930s and then returned to Houston. There he opened the famous Bronze Peacock Dinner Club in 1945, booking some of the top jazz bands and orchestras to play, leading to immense success. With his assistant Evelyn Johnson (see this cemetery's entry), Robey opened record stores and had started the Buffalo Booking Agency by 1950. His first client was twenty-three-year-old singer/guitarist Clarence "Gatemouth" Brown. When he became dissatisfied with the way Aladdin Records was handling his client, Robey decided to start his own record company, Peacock Records, in 1949.

Over the years, he would add artists such as Memphis Slim, Floyd Dixon, Little Richard and Willie Mae "Big Mama" Thornton, whose 1953 recording of "Hound Dog" became a top hit. When he added a gospel division to the company, it became one of the leading gospel labels in the United States, leading to a second gospel label, Song Bird, in 1963–64.

Robey closed the Bronze Peacock Club in the mid-1950s after gaining full control of a partnership with the Duke record label, establishing both labels in the club's space and bringing onto his label Bobby "Blue" Bland, his most consistent artist, with thirty-six songs reaching the Billboard R&B charts between 1957 and 1970. Other labels under his guidance would form, transform and be sold, and due to his shrewd (some say deceitful) business practices and dealings with artists, he is credited with a substantial role in the development of Texas blues and its musicians. He was also a leader in multiple local organizations such as the NAACP, chamber of commerce and YMCA among others.

Notable Resident: Evelyn Joyce Johnson

The Queen of Rhythm and Blues, Evelyn Joyce Johnson (1920–2005), served as business manager of Don Robey's Duke-Peacock recording empire in Houston as well as president of the Buffalo Booking Agency. From the late 1940s until 1973, Johnson worked to create, develop and operate one of the United States' most commercially successful African American–owned and operated music businesses of the mid-twentieth century. This enterprise would ultimately include at least five record labels, a music publishing company and an extremely powerful and influential booking agency. During this time, several up-and-coming blues, R&B, gospel and pop artists found themselves associated with Johnson's direction as they worked to establish themselves as major stars.

Even in death, the two professionals changed the way the music industry in Houston worked. Evelyn Johnson lies mere feet from Don Robey. Acts such as Little Richard, Big Mama Thornton, Gatemouth Brown, the Original Five Blind Boys and a young B.B. King all felt the influence of these two music icons. *Author's collection.*

Johnson grew up in the Fifth Ward, graduating from Phillis Wheatley High School and going on to work as an X-ray technician while studying at Houston College for Negros (now Texas Southern University). Then, in 1946, she took a job as the office manager at the Bronze Peacock, a Fifth Ward nightclub operated by Don Robey. One night in 1947, the relatively unknown guitarist and blues singer Clarence "Gatemouth" Brown replaced the esteemed T-Bone Walker onstage, delivering a firestorm of a performance that led to Robey working with Johnson to sign the artist to a management contract. Following this, Johnson completely retooled the independent recording industry as Peacock Records, got her license to book and manage union artists, made herself president and became one of the few African Americans to compete directly with White-owned booking agencies at the time. This operation would bring on the Original Five Blind Boys, Floyd Dixon and Willie Mae "Big Mama" Thornton and acquire Duke Records and its roster in 1952, adding Johnny Ace and Bobby Bland plus a young B.B. King. Robey and Johnson would go on to add Back Beat and Song Bird in 1957 and 1963, respectively.

Johnson remained in charge of the office through 1973, when Robey sold all his music-related assets and retired. In her later years, Johnson chose to stay in Houston. She worked in real estate and banking prior to her own retirement and remained active in Houston. She died in 2005, never married with no children. Shortly before her death, Project Row Houses celebrated her achievements by staging a Duke-Peacock Reunion concert in her honor at Houston's historic Eldorado Ballroom.

Notable Resident: Hobart Taylor Sr.

Born to a former slave turned entrepreneur and landowner, Hobart Taylor Sr. (1890–1972) became an influential mover in Houston's civil rights movement. His father, Jack Taylor, died when Hobart was five, eventually leaving him two thousand acres of farmland in Fort Bend and Wharton Counties. Taylor would graduate from Prairie View, go to insurance school and secure a job at Atlanta's Standard Life Insurance Company. He became the first salesman to write up $1 million worth of business in a single year—a short-lived accomplishment as when the Great Depression hit, the insurance business in Texas sank. Taylor used his entrepreneurial skills, along with some inherited money, to purchase a Houston taxicab franchise.

Due to Jim Crow laws, Taylor was restricted to Black neighborhoods, but Houston was a hub for African Americans migrating during World War II and into the 1950s. By the time of his death, Taylor's business was worth multimillions, a financial empire that involved real estate—including that farmland his father left him, now dotted with oil wells. Taylor also funded a court case to include African Americans in Texas primaries in 1944, was an early major contributor to the United Negro College Fund, supported Lyndon B. Johnson for the Senate in 1948 and was a Texas delegate to the 1956 National Democratic Convention. He and his son, prominent Detroit attorney Hobart Taylor Jr., were early supporters of LBJ's bid for the White House in 1960.

Chapter 22

ST. VINCENT'S CEMETERY

2400 Navigation Boulevard Houston

Located on the north side of Navigation Boulevard, St. Vincent's Cemetery is in an increasingly gentrified neighborhood just east of downtown. The cemetery is within sight of the Esplanade on Navigation Boulevard and just down the street from the original famed restaurant Ninfa's on Navigation. Parking at the cemetery is difficult, but there is street parking and lot parking nearby.

HISTORY

Located next to Our Lady of Guadalupe Church, St. Vincent's Cemetery was established in 1853, sixty years prior to the church. It is located in the East End of Houston, an area settled by immigrants, and the headstones reflect that, carved with German, Italian, French and other nationalities' surnames. The congregation, St. Vincent de Paul, held its first mass in 1842 at a church located at Franklin and Caroline but owned this land for years prior to relocating its church here.

The property had been purchased from a tract of land from the estate of local businessman and philanthropist John Kennedy, who is buried in this cemetery along with his family. The cemetery holds many unmarked graves, including numerous burials from an 1867 yellow fever epidemic. Around 1911, a great influx of refugees from Mexico arrived in the East End due to

For years, visitors to Houston's East End could see how important St. Vincent's Cemetery was with the existence of this metal sign looking over Navigation Boulevard. It reads: "St. Vincent's Cemetery. Founded 1852. Burial place of Dick Dowling, hero of Sabine Pass; Samuel Paschal, hero of San Jacinto; and other Houston pioneers." *Author's collection.*

unrest in their country. The church began in 1912, with a school following that fall. It served Houston until 1927 and is the oldest Catholic cemetery in Houston. The City of Houston condemned the cemetery in 1871, but the last burial did not take place until a Polish count was buried here in 1927; the diocese now takes care of the property, which is in good repair and generally well maintained.

Memorable Headstones

In 1949, a monument made from Texas granite was erected inside the cemetery. This monument honors those "fallen heroes of San Jacinto and Sabine Pass" who were buried in St. Vincent's. One side tells the story of Santa Anna's defeat, while the other briefly recounts Lieutenant Dowling's exploits. Time and weather have smoothed the stone somewhat, making deciphering of the heroes of the battles listed difficult. Inadequate records help muddy those facts.

The monument erected in St. Vincent's to the fallen heroes of San Jacinto and Sabine Pass mark two of the highwater marks for the area's military history. One side recounts the story of Santa Anna's defeat, while another recounts the exploits of Dick Dowling at the Battle of Sabine Pass. *Author's collection.*

Local Celebrities

Samuel Paschal (1815–1874) was born and raised in Kentucky and lived in Little Rock, Arkansas, before emigrating to Texas in 1836. He arrived at Velasco, having been recruited for the regular army of Texas by Captain Amasa Turner in New Orleans. He was in Captain Turner's company at San Jacinto, earning land on his return for serving the republic, and after the war, he settled in Houston as a cabinetmaker and carpenter. He was among the vice presidents later chosen during a convention endorsing General Sam Houston for president of the United States.

Notable Resident: Dick Dowling

Richard William Dowling (1837–1867), native of Ireland, became famous for his actions during the Civil War, becoming the "Hero of Sabine Pass." In 1863, Lieutenant Dick Dowling commanded Fort Griffin with forty-six men. Located on Sabine Pass, near present-day Port Arthur, the location served as a primary Texas port for Confederate shipments of supplies and was vital in their war effort. In a battle lasting less than an hour, Dowling and his men managed to destroy two gunboats, which resulted in significant casualties and the subsequent capture of nearly 350 prisoners. Thanks to Dowling's efforts, the area ports escaped capture; Union forces never penetrated the Texas interior during the war. For his efforts, he was promoted to major and spent the remainder of the war traveling and recruiting troops for the state, having instantly become a hero beyond just his hometown of Houston.

Following the war, Dowling returned to his saloon business in Houston, joined several civic organizations and served with a Houston volunteer fire department, becoming one of the city's leading businessmen. However, this promising start to a postwar career was abruptly cut short. In 1867, at the age of thirty, Dowling contracted yellow fever and died. His Houston Hook & Ladder Company carried him to his final resting place in St. Vincent's. Despite a light rain, thousands lined the streets to see him off.

NOTABLE RESIDENT: JOHN KENNEDY

Irish immigrant and early Houston businessman John Kennedy (1819–1878) arrived in Houston during the Republic of Texas years. The family lived in what is now downtown Houston, east of the Main Street Market Square district in an area called Quality Hill, a short distance from Kennedy's bakery business. His business and real estate holdings placed him in the upper echelon of wealthy Houstonians. He deeded land to the Catholic Church to construct a church downtown and, at one time, owned all the buildings on the north side of the 800 block of Congress, including his own Steam Bakery Building at 813 Congress.

People traipsing through the bars and restaurants in Houston's Market Square probably wonder a little about the old brick building now called La Carafe. Old, candlelit, tilting a bit off kilter—just a different little pocket than the rest of its neighbors. John Kennedy, Irish immigrant and early Houston businessman, ran his Steam Bakery Building here at 813 Congress. It is the oldest building still being used commercially in the city. *Author's collection.*

When the Civil War hit, Kennedy continued to be involved in a wide range of business ventures and to operate his bakery, possibly entering a contract with the Confederate government to produce hardtack, a durable, bread-like provision used by both armies. He also leased space in one of these buildings to the ordinance officer of the District of Texas, New Mexico and Arizona for use as a munitions factory and storehouse. As the war ended, and it was feared that Houston would fall to the Union, the warehouse was ordered abandoned and the munitions promptly sunk in Buffalo Bayou.

Following the war, Kennedy operated a steam gristmill and rented out space in his buildings for a variety of purposes, primarily grocery stores and the printing business. The last mention of the building's use as a bakery was in 1870, when his son John Jr. was operating the business; he would eventually inherit it. On Christmas Eve 1878, John Kennedy was murdered outside the doors of the Kennedy Corner Building. Today, his bakery building houses the longtime Houston bar La Carafe.

Chapter 23

WASHINGTON CEMETERY

2911 Washington Avenue
Houston

Located adjacent to one of Houston's most spectacular and expansive cemeteries is the old Deutsche Gesellschaft von Houston's German Society Cemetery, now known better as Washington Cemetery. While the only access is through its neighbor to the east, Glenwood Cemetery, this is still an active cemetery with over 7,500 burials covering over thirteen acres.

History

Houston's German society organization Deutsche Gesellschaft von Houston was founded in 1875, bringing together Houston's strong German immigrant population. It began offering family lots and singles spaces on their cemetery land, established in 1887, to the public. It was a popular cemetery among Houston's immigrants, with at least seventeen countries represented in its grounds. Gravestones here can be found inscribed in not only English and German but also Spanish, Polish and other European languages. When sentiments toward Germans in U.S. cities throughout the country became negative around the time of World War I, the cemetery changed its name to Washington Cemetery.

While in continuous use, the cemetery eventually began to fall into neglect. Following the murder of Leona Tonn, the caretaker living on the property, in 1977, volunteer citizens banded together, deciding that something needed

Above: When Glenwood took over management of Washington Cemetery, it connected the two in their pathways more seamlessly. In doing so, it eliminated the need for a separate entry to the old German cemetery. Despite this, the original entry and gate remain and can be seen, almost hidden, along the drives of Washington Avenue. *Author's collection.*

Left: In 1999, Washington Cemetery merged with its neighbor Glenwood Cemetery. When it did, it transferred the right to restore, operate and maintain the property as a historic cemetery to Glenwood. With more integration between the two properties, Glenwood erected these markers to show the delineation between the two. *Author's collection.*

to be done about the property. From 1977 until 1999, Washington Cemetery was restored, operated and maintained. In 1999, the group merged with Glenwood Cemetery, transferring the right to restore, operate and maintain their property as a historic cemetery.

Local Celebrities

Hugh Hamilton (1853–1922) built the city's first ice plant, developing a process of making clear ice from Houston's artesian water. Along with fellow businessmen, he established the Magnolia Brewery, later known as the Magnolia Dairy Products Company. His Central Texas Ice, Light & Water Company operated numerous plants throughout the state. He also served four terms as a city alderman in the First Ward from 1886 to 1894.

Ernest Heinrich Holdgraf (1867–1950) and Emma K. Marti Holdgraf (1875–1937) were part owners of a traveling tent show known as the Jolly Rovers. Emma worked as a buck-and-wing dancer in the show. Later, the couple operated amusement parks at Magnolia and Highland Parks while also managing the food concessions for the Houston Buffaloes Baseball Stadiums. The Holdgrafs introduced potato chips to Houstonians, eventually selling the operation to the Dentler Brothers, who produced the Dentler-Maid Potato Chip.

James J. Hussey (1865–1941) served Houston as fire chief from 1898 to 1901, with an office located in Station 7, the city's first true Houston Fire Department station house. Prior to the construction of this building, the city utilized older volunteer force buildings, but this new one was designed for the new paid service. While it was one of several stations serving Houston, Chief Hussey managed the horse-drawn fire vehicles and men to protect Houston's nine square miles and 44,633 residents. The station still stands at 2403 Milam and serves as the Fire Museum of Houston.

Henry F. Jonas (1868–1948) was an architect of the firm Henry F. Jonas & Tabor. Jonas's firm designed many structures now considered historic, including the Butler Brothers Building, the Third Church of Christ, Scientist, and the Texan Theater. However, Jonas's crowning achievement—and likely his best known—was Houston's Buffalo Stadium, home to the minor league baseball Buffs from 1928 to 1961. When it was built, it was considered state of the art, including a Spanish-style tiled-roof entryway and large plaques of buffaloes on the wall around the stadium.

John Dickson "Peck" Kelley (1898–1980) was a jazz pianist and bandleader best known for his 1920s band Peck's Bad Boys, featuring the likes of Louis Prima, Jack Teagarden and Pee Wee Russell. Peck himself played for the silent movies in the Texan, Palace and Majestic Theaters downtown, while his band was often a fixture at parties held in the Rice Hotel and at the island's Balinese Room. He repeatedly turned down offers to play outside of Texas with musicians such as Bing Crosby, the Dorseys and Paul Whiteman. Despite a few performances early on in Missouri and Louisiana, he seems to have stuck to Texas. In the 1950s, Peck joined the Dick Shannon quartet, a period from which the only recordings of his work have survived. Kelley was an intensely private man and did not seek out fame. Eventually, he became blind and suffered from Parkinson's Disease before dying in 1980 at the age of eighty-two. In 1983, following his long refusal to have recordings of his work published, Commodore Records released *Peck Valley Jam Session, Volume 1 and 2*.

Notable Resident: Charles August Albert Dellschau

Charles August Albert Dellschau (1830–1923) was a retired butcher who is posthumously viewed as a legitimate artist. Dellschau wrote a two-hundred-page journal along with several notebooks. Within those pages are some five thousand ink-and-watercolor drawings of elaborate flying machines. He is viewed as one of America's earliest-known visionary artists, a style that purports to transcend the physical world and portrays, or bases itself in, a wider vision of awareness including spiritual or mystical themes. Little is known about Dellschau's life, especially before his emigration from Prussia to Texas in 1850. However, following his retirement in 1899, he worked on his art in the attic apartment of his stepdaughter and her husband in Houston until his death at the age of ninety-three.

Dellschau's artwork was almost lost for good, first as it languished in the home and again following a 1960s fire, when the artwork was placed on the curb as trash. A local antiques dealer managed to snare the notebooks and eventually showed them to Houston art patron and collector Dominique de Menil, who purchased four of the notebooks for $1,500. Later, seven

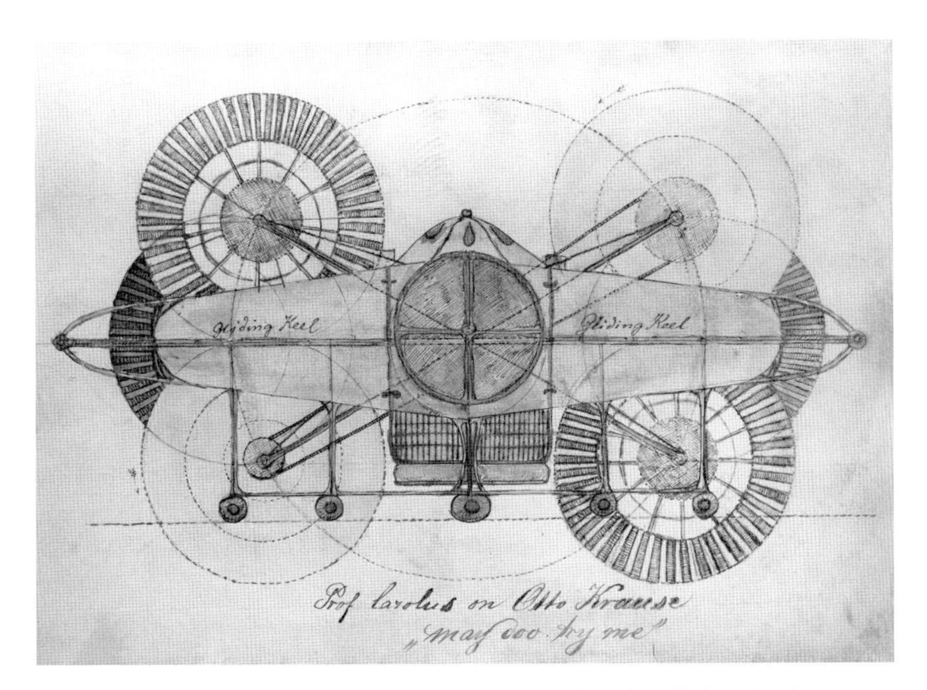

One of Charles Dellschau's elaborate "Aeros." The retired butcher filled notebooks with elaborate flying machines, but it wasn't until after his death that he was viewed as a legitimate artist. Today, his work can be found hanging in various museum galleries. *Courtesy of Library of Congress.*

were purchased by Pete Navarro, a Houston commercial artist and UFO researcher, who later sold four to museums in San Antonio. Dellschau's "Aeros" can now be seen in San Antonio's Museum of Art and the Witte Museum.

NOTABLE RESIDENT: EUGENE HEINER

Renowned Texas architect Eugene Heinger (1852–1901) was born in New York City and, as a teenager, studied to be an architect in Chicago before moving to Dallas in 1877 and to Houston the following year. A bit of a wunderkind from the start, Heiner won a design competition and earned a commission early on to design the Galveston County Jailhouse. He is considered Houston's first professional architect and his impact is easily noticed.

Over the next two decades, Heiner became well known for designing almost forty Texas jails and courthouses, many of which are listed on the National Register of Historic Places. Heiner also designed a building on the campus of Texas A&M in College Station and one at the Texas State Penitentiary in Huntsville.

Heiner's design work wasn't limited to jails and courthouses, though, and his legacy is visible through numerous commissions executed throughout Galveston and Houston, with designs ranging from Italianate to Romanesque to American High Victorian. Some of the best-known buildings in Galveston bearing his mark are the Blum Building and the Kaufman & Runge Building. In Houston, some of his more notable works include the Houston Cotton Exchange, the Sweeney & Coombs Opera House, the Henry Brashear Building and the W.L. Foley Building. Additional works of his can be found throughout the state.

Notable Resident: Sarah Emma Evelyn Edmonds Seelye, a.k.a. Frank Thompson

Sarah Emma Edmonds Seelye (1841–1898), better known to fellow soldiers as Franklin Flint Thompson, was one of the few females known to have served during the Civil War. Born in Canada and facing an abusive father and a forced marriage, Sarah Edmonds fled to Flint, Michigan, in 1856. To hide from her father, travel undetected and secure a job, she disguised herself as a man and took the name Franklin Thompson.

When the Civil War struck, she felt compelled to join the military out of a sense of duty and enlisted as a male field nurse in the Second Michigan Infantry. As Franklin Flint Thompson, she participated in several battles during 1862 in Maryland, including Second Manassas and Antietam, dealing with mass casualties in her role. She was also present at the Siege of Yorktown and the battles at Williamsburg, Fair Oaks, Malvern Hill and Fredericksburg.

While there is no official record, she is also said to have served as a Union spy, infiltrating the Confederate army several times. Her alleged aliases included a Southern sympathizer named Charles Mayberry; Bridget

Opposite: Sarah Edmonds escaped abuse and resentment at the hands of her father, who longed to have a son. She fled Canada for the United States and, feeling the urge to serve her new home, enlisted as Franklin Thompson in the Union Army. She was present at battles such as Malvern Hill, Fredericksburg, Second Manassas and Antietam and also reportedly served as a spy. *Courtesy of National Archives.*

Above: When Sarah Edmonds died, she had long since laid to rest the persona of Franklin Thompson. However, she had eventually been awarded an honorable discharge and a pension and admitted as the Grand Army of the Republic's only female member. In 1901, she was moved from her grave site in La Porte to the Grand Army of the Republic section of Washington Cemetery with full military honors. *Author's collection.*

O'Shea, an Irish peddler selling soap and apples; and a Black man named Cuff, using wigs and silver nitrate to dye her skin as a disguise.

When she contracted malaria, she first requested a furlough, which was denied. Realizing the gig was up, she gave up her military career. She knew if she went to a military hospital for treatment, she would be discovered—and conversely, becoming a deserter on leaving made it impossible for her to return following recovery. On recovery, though, she continued as a nurse, this time as herself at a hospital for soldiers in Washington, D.C.

She published an account of her experiences in 1865, married, had children and was eventually awarded an honorable discharge from the military, given a government pension and admitted to the Grand Army of the Republic as the order's only female member. In September

1898, due to complications from the malaria she contracted in 1863, Edmonds died in La Porte at the age of fifty-six. She was buried in the local cemetery but later laid to rest a second time—this time, in 1901, with full military honors in the Grand Army of the Republic section of Washington Cemetery.

Chapter 24

WOODLAWN CEMETERY

1101 Antoine Drive
Houston

Enter Woodlawn from one of two entrances, one on Katy Road and the other on Antoine. Both entrances are framed by double wrought-iron gates. The Katy option is located next to the abandoned Missouri-Katy-Texas Railroad tracks, while next to the Antoine entry is the Beth Israel Cemetery, which forms part of Woodlawn's eastern boundary.

History

Founded on a rural plot of land on the far western edge of Houston in 1931, which was once nearly two miles outside the city limits, this peaceful enclave of sixty acres, much of it heavily forested, now rests surrounded by the din of a bustling city. When developed, it was surrounded by farmland and the main road, Katy Freeway, was simply a dirt road. Farmers would frequently drive cattle away from funeral services taking place. So primitive was the site that it housed only a small field office at the cemetery; formal operations were conducted out of the J.S. Cullinan Petroleum Building downtown.

Today, roads wind through a mix of aboveground monuments and flat burial markers. There is very limited planned landscaping. Burials until 1940 were all marked with upright tombstones. Following that, flat bronze markers were specified for the other sections of the cemetery. Any remaining

Woodlawn Cemetery started out on a rural plot of land on the far western edge of town back in 1931. What once was a two-mile trek outside the city limits is today surrounded by city and just off one of Houston's busiest thoroughfares, Interstate 10. *Author's collection.*

sections either have a combo of both upright and flat or consist entirely of the newer flat markers, such as Babyland, Cupid's Heart, Garden of the Last Supper and Garden of the Praying Hands.

Memorable Headstones: Annie Laurie Wishing Chair

The chair, made of imitation cut stone, is a copy of Dionicio Rodriguez's own original, located in the forecourt of a church in Scotland. It is noted, through a plaque on the chair, that legend states "if a couple sits in the chair on their wedding day, holds hands and makes a wish, it will come true."

Local Celebrity

David F. Lock (1920–2015) stood as one of Houston's last known Pearl Harbor survivors. He had joined the marines while working in the Civilian Conservation Corps to help his family in Florida during the Great Depression.

The Annie Laurie Wishing Chair can be found not only at Woodlawn but also at Forest Lawn in Hollywood as well as others. In fact, the original sits on display at a church in Scotland. Annie Laurie was a seventeenth-century Scottish woman whom William Douglas fell in love with, writing a poem in her honor. The story is that if a bride and groom sit on the chair and recite a Scottish wedding poem, their marriage will be filled with good luck. *Author's collection.*

After boot camp in San Diego, he was stationed aboard the USS *Pennsylvania*, which was dry-docked on that fateful December 7, 1941 morning. Armed with just a .50-caliber machine gun, he fired on Japanese warplanes as they came into view. Following the war, he raised his family in the Heights area and worked in the refineries in Pasadena.

NOTABLE RESIDENT: JULISSA D'ANNE GOMEZ

Julissa d'Anne Gomez (1972–1991) was a rising star in women's gymnastics. She was born in San Antonio and honed her skills in Texas since she was ten years old with famed gymnastics trainers Bela Karolyi and Al Fong. Scheduled to compete in the 1988 Worlds Sports Fair in Tokyo, an event held prior to the 1988 U.S. Olympic Trials, Gomez performed well from the outset and qualified for the vault finals.

The following day, Gomez began warming up by practicing her weakest vault, an extremely difficult and dangerous maneuver called the Yurchenko Vault. In her transition from running to vaulting, she missed the springboard, hitting her head on the vaulting horse and breaking her neck in the process. She was immediately tended to and transported to a nearby hospital. Paralyzed from the neck down, she was placed on a respirator. A week later, doctors performed a tracheotomy to help her breathe on her own, yet she remained on the respirator, with oxygen supplied to her. However, a mishap the following day led to her being disconnected from her respirator and oxygen supply overnight. Gomez lapsed into a coma, resulting in considerable brain damage. She eventually contracted a lethal infection in 1991.

Due to Gomez's vault accident, major changes were made in the field of gymnastics. The vaulting horse was replaced with a vaulting table. The springboard was modified as well, to prevent such an accident from ever happening again. Probably the most important change came in the code of points. Any participant to attempt the Yurchenko Vault without the use of the new equipment would suffer an automatic score of zero, effectively an immediate disqualification.

Julissa Gomez was a rising star in the world of gymnastics and likely to be a medalist at the 1988 Olympics. She began her day practicing her weakest vault, the Yurchenko Vault. In missing the springboard, she broke her neck, paralyzing her. In a series of events that followed, she entered a coma, never to awaken. *Courtesy of Library of Congress.*

NOTABLE RESIDENT: MARVIN ZINDLER

Houston has some colorful characters peppering its backstory. Likely one of the most notorious on that list would be former journalist Marvin Zindler (1921–2007). In 1943, he took a part-time radio gig as a DJ and spot news reporter for KATL (currently MKIC 1590). Later, he would add newspaper reporter, cameraman, crime reporter and photographer to his résumé. Building on this extensive experience, Zindler stepped into the field of investigative reporting, working for Harris County in the sheriff's office and district court office.

Marvin would return to the media in 1973, joining KTRK-AM. During this stint, Marvin Zindler became famous, making local and national

Marvin Zindler was a KTRK-TV news reporter whose investigative journalism made him one of Houston's most influential and well-known media personalities. He was a pioneer of consumer reporting and served Houston's public, especially the elderly and indigent, for over three decades. *Courtesy of Special Collections, University of Houston Libraries.*

headlines through his work with Larry Conners, most notably regarding a long-lived brothel near La Grange called the Chicken Ranch. Zindler wouldn't stop there; his Rat and Roach Report had him reading details from his controversial City of Houston Food Inspection Program on the air with reports of "sliiiiiime in the ice machine!" Many restaurants throughout Houston would eventually make at least one appearance, including KTRK's own commissary.

It wasn't all uncovering the seedy side of Houston. Zindler also was well known through his investigations in helping the elderly and the working class and created a path to help charity patients who needed assistance for reconstructive surgery. Zindler would be diagnosed with inoperable pancreatic cancer, finding that it had spread to his liver. Two nights after signing off from what would be his final newscast, Marvin Zindler died. His funeral took place at Congregation Beth Israel before heading next door to be interred at Woodlawn.

Special Features

Dionicio Rodriguez was a Mexican-born artist and architect whose work can be found in multiple states, Washington D.C. and Mexico City as well as throughout Texas, where he is buried. His work is noted for its unique style of concrete construction that imitates wood through a process known as faux bois (French for "false wood"). He designed gates, benches and artificial rock formations that invite visitors to rest or explore the landscape. His fifteen works throughout Woodlawn, installed around 1940, are the only known extant cemetery work by Rodriguez in the state and are listed on the National Register of Historic Places. Of the pieces, one is a twenty-five-foot cross made of four cross-sawn timbers resting on a two-tiered base of other timbers. It features peeling bark, insect holes and knot holes and is surrounded by four complementary benches.

Rodriguez's other sculptures include a woven basket, additional benches, a mound-shaped honeycomb rock fountain and the Annie Laurie Wishing Tree. Another highlight is a single textured "trunk" that splits, with two

Works by Dionicio Rodriguez can be found interspersed throughout Woodland. The Mexican-born artist and architect's work can be found in multiple states, especially in Texas. His process is known as faux bois, French for "false wood," and his designs resemble gates, benches and artificial rock formations. This bench resembles a fallen tree and includes fine details right down to the bark. *Author's collection.*

pieces forming the back of a bench and seat, stumps working as legs and the trunk emerging out of the ground. The cross feature is not replicated anywhere else in his work, and the latter feature, the fallen tree branch, is often repeated but exists here as the longest example that he sculpted.

ABOUT THE AUTHOR

Courtesy of Tristan Smith.

Tristan Smith is an independent historian living in Houston, Texas. He has worked for museums and nonprofits in Kansas, Missouri and Texas for over twenty years in marketing, curation, education, volunteer, management and administrative capacities. Museums he's been involved with have featured natural history, the 1950s, fine art, community history, a sunken steamboat found in a Kansas cornfield, a United States president and firefighting history. He has also consulted for organizations and municipalities in historic preservation. He is the author of *Houston Fire Department* (Images of America series; Arcadia Publishing, 2015) and *A History Lover's Guide to Houston* (The History Press, 2020). His additional work can be found on his website, www.thehistorysmith.com.